Dear Reader:

The book you are about to rea[...]
Martin's True Crime Library, t[...]
"the leader in true crime!" Eac[...]...inating
account of the latest, most sensational crime that has captured the
national attention. St. Martin's is the publisher of bestselling true
crime author and crime journalist Kieran Crowley, who explores
the dark, deadly links between a prominent Manhattan surgeon
and the disappearance of his wife fifteen years earlier in THE
SURGEON'S WIFE. Suzy Spencer's BREAKING POINT guides readers
through the tortuous twists and turns in the case of Andrea Yates,
the Houston mother who drowned her five young children in the
family's bathtub. In Edgar Award-nominated DARK DREAMS, legendary FBI profiler Roy Hazelwood and bestselling crime author
Stephen G. Michaud shine light on the inner workings of America's
most violent and depraved murderers. In the book you now hold,
KILLER BODIES, acclaimed author Michael Fleeman takes you into
the lives of a bodybuilding couple with a dark secret.

St. Martin's True Crime Library gives you the stories behind the
headlines. Our authors take you right to the scene of the crime and
into the minds of the most notorious murderers to show you what
really makes them tick. St. Martin's True Crime Library paperbacks are better than the most terrifying thriller, because it's all
true! The next time you want a crackling good read, make sure it's
got the St. Martin's True Crime Library logo on the spine—you'll
be up all night!

Charles E. Spicer, Jr.

Charles E. Spicer, Jr.
Executive Editor, St. Martin's True Crime Library

ST. MARTIN'S TRUE CRIME LIBRARY TITLES
BY MICHAEL FLEEMAN

LACI

"IF I DIE..."

THE STRANGER IN MY BED

OVER THE EDGE

DEADLY MISTRESS

KILLER BODIES

A GLAMOROUS BODYBUILDING COUPLE, A LOVE TRIANGLE, AND A BRUTAL MURDER

MICHAEL FLEEMAN

St. Martin's Paperbacks

KILLER BODIES

Copyright © 2007 by Michael Fleeman.

Cover photo of dumbbells © Hans Neleman/zefa/Corbis. Cover photo of Kelly Ryan © Bill Dobbins. Cover photo of Craig Titus © Gary Gardiner.

ISBN: 0-312-94202-8
EAN: 9780312-94202-1

Printed in the United States of America

St. Martin's Paperbacks edition / September 2007

St. Martin's Paperbacks are published by St. Martin's Press, 175 Fifth Avenue, New York, NY 10010.

10 9 8 7 6 5 4 3 2 1

KILLER BODIES

The phone rang.

It was her ex-husband, Dennis James, the car salesman who lived in Florida. He had just received a call from a woman in the coroner's office in Las Vegas.

She was asking about Melissa, their daughter.

CHAPTER ONE

THE FIRE COULD BE SEEN FOR MILES, BURNING IN the black nothingness of the desert. A frigid December wind had kicked up, temperatures hovering just above freezing, sand and dust blowing everywhere.

There's a reason they called this Sandy Valley Road.

One gust and the tinder-dry brush could catch fire, and then Dick Draper would be in trouble. As it was, his fire truck was running low on water and foam. The burning Jaguar was all blistering red paint and collapsing roof, a crackling, flaming skeleton.

Draper wanted to keep the fire right where it was, on a bluff at the end of a wash, in the middle of nowhere—the valley on the other other side of the "hump to Pahrump," as the locals called the mountains that separate Las Vegas from the closest town where hooking is legal.

A trucker rumbling down Route 160 called this one in about 4:30 a.m. He could see the fire from the highway, barely a quarter mile away, in the morning darkness. Las Vegas Metro dispatch relayed the call to the closest fire department, the Mountain Springs volunteers, headed by Draper.

He responded himself in his truck loaded with water and foam.

The drive from his home at the Mountain Springs summit took Draper down a sharp incline that opened to a vast desert floor, the dim lights of Pahrump's homes, stores and brothels twinkling in the distance.

As the road leveled, the fire came into view a few hundred yards off the highway.

Draper pulled his truck off at the Sandy Valley sign and hit a bumpy, barely graded, undercarriage-shredding road full of rocks and deep holes. He negotiated around the worst of the dips to the end of the wash, where the Jaguar blazed like Christmas, just eleven days away.

Draper opened his truck door and was hit by a blast of winter-in-the-desert temperature: 34 degrees that morning.

As he readied the hose to spray down the flames, Draper noticed that the fire was moving from the rear of the car to the front, with flames shooting from the back seat and heading toward the hood, taking out the roof along the way. This was fortunate. The fire was going away from the gas tank in the back.

Draper unleashed a spray of water to keep the fire from spreading to the brush. After a few minutes, he had things sufficiently under control to switch to the foam to fully extinguish the blaze, including the burning magnesium car parts, which can't be put out with mere water.

After forty-five minutes, Draper had run out of water and foam. The once-roaring fire had been reduced to a charred car skeleton with a few glowing hot spots. Draper believed the blaze had been contained enough for him to leave the scene for his base atop the mountain and get another truck with more water and foam.

The trip there and back took less than twenty minutes—it was after 5 a.m. by now—and Draper again went to work, dousing the remaining stubborn areas. Having responded to dozens of car fires in the desert, Draper knew the car had to be cool before the tow truck could safely take it away. He poured water and foam all over a section in the middle of the car, but the smoke kept coming.

Working in the darkness, he poked at the area with a pole, stirring the ashes, and sprayed it some more.

It was slow work and Draper struggled to see. He got out his flashlight and directed the beam toward the rear of the car.

That's when he first saw the body, lying on its side, in what used to be the trunk, only now was a cavity separated from the back seat area by nothing, the fire having destroyed the barrier.

The flashlight beam shined on a head swaddled in cloth, then landed on a blackened hand.

Draper put his pike back in the truck and dialed dispatch, asking them to alert Metro.

THE HOMICIDE UNIT OF THE LAS VEGAS METROPOLitan Police Department got the call at 6:31 a.m. on December 14, 2005. The detectives on duty that morning were Robert Wilson, Clifford Mogg, Ken Hardy and Dean O'Kelley. The rotation had O'Kelley up as the lead investigator.

Their supervisor, Sergeant Rocky Alby, briefed them: a car fire in the desert west of Las Vegas, with an apparent victim in the trunk. The report came from a volunteer fireman who had put out the blaze and then found the body. No known witnesses, nothing else to report.

As dawn broke on what would be a crisp, clear winter day in southern Nevada, the detectives headed for Pahrump. The drive took them west on Blue Diamond Highway, on the fringe of Vegas, where the desert is fighting a losing battle against the bulldozer. On both sides of the highway, housing tracks are sprouting, miles of identical stucco boxes with Spanish-tiled roofs, advertised on billboards with names like "Trail Ridge" and "Parkview Estates," despite the absence of any obvious trails, ridges, parks or views. Realtors' flags in red and yellow strain against the fierce desert winds.

By day, so many construction trucks clog Blue Diamond Highway that traffic backs up for a half-mile or more at intersections closest to the Interstate 15 on-ramp, itself a work in progress, plunged into a major renovation.

But at this hour—shortly before 7 a.m.—traffic was light and the detectives made good time.

Soon, the highway narrowed, and the construction zones gave way to the desert. In the distance to the north, the jagged outcroppings of Red Rock Canyon rose and the road signs warned, "LOOK OUT FOR WILD HORSES AND BURROS ON HIGHWAY." The road twisted and rose up into the mountains, the desert scrub replaced by cool pines. In the rearview: miles of housing tracks and the towering gambling palaces of The Strip, just now shaking off its daily hangover.

After the 5,490-foot Mountain Springs summit,

where Dick Draper made his base, the road dipped down to a valley floor. From there, it was a couple miles to the turnoff to Sandy Valley, with the fire scene just off the highway.

The trip from Vegas took about a half-hour, something to keep in mind for a time line in a homicide investigation.

ARRIVING AT THE SCENE, THE FOUR METRO DETECtives found the charred remains of the 2003 Jaguar on the side of the graded road, the ground around it muddied by the water and foam. This once-lonely spot in the desert started buzzing with activity. Additional fire trucks would arrive, as would squad cars and vehicles for the coroner and crime-scene analysts.

The detectives received a briefing from Dick Draper about how he had put out the fire and found the body while dousing the hot spots. Draper led them to car, now little more than a darkened frame, the fire having peeled away the paint and blown out the windows, headlights and taillights. Red molding had fallen to the ground, as had the back license plate, burnt so badly that only the number 9 and the letters PPL remained.

What appeared to be shoe marks had been pressed into the dry ground, but they were of little evidentiary value now because the wind had filled them with dirt and sand. There were fading tire marks, an old beer can and other garbage in the brush, all of it old and weathered and unrelated to the case.

The car held all the evidence they would find. In the front seat area lay a blackened flashlight, and nearby, broken pieces from the light littered the ground. In the back sat the last vestiges of a burned suitcase—just the frame—surrounded by its former contents: blackened clothing, keys, tweezers, ceramic salt and pepper shakers, barbecue tools, makeup case, burnt food and syringes.

The ignition held no keys, nor were any to be found.

The trunk lid was locked, so the detectives pried the metal away with a crowbar. Inside the trunk cavity were the fire-ravaged remnants of material: scraps of a fleece blanket dyed purple, blue and black, a second blanket with what looked like a tiger print in orange and black, and a thick off-white cotton fabric.

Beneath the blankets lay the body, clad in a blue hooded sweatshirt, denim jeans, and red panties visible through the burned-out holes in the jeans. The head was facing the passenger side, the left arm folded under the torso, a metal bracelet around the wrist.

No face was visible. A woven fabric covered the head with only wisps of reddish-brown hair visible where the cloth had burned away. A wire was wrapped around the neck, like a ligature.

Based on the size and build of the body and what little remained of the clothing, it appeared to be that of a young woman or older girl.

The fire had claimed any personal identification, such as a passport or driver's license, if any had existed.

The car's owner couldn't be immediately determined, as registration papers had perished and flames had destroyed the Vehicle Identification Number plate and much of the license plate.

But in talking to Draper, it turns out that before the fire had gotten too out of control, the volunteer chief had taken the time to write down the license plate number. A check with the motor vehicle department found that the Jaguar was registered to Kelly Ann Ryan, a 33-year-old woman who lived on Adobe Arch Road in Las Vegas.

Lead Detective O'Kelley stayed at the fire scene to continue investigating. The three other detectives—Robert Wilson, Cliff Mogg and Ken Hardy—headed back to the city to the home of the car's owner, whose physical description, as reported on her driver's license, matched that of the body in the car.

The detectives prepared themselves for what could turn out to be a death notification to Ms. Ryan's next of kin.

AT THE SAME TIME THE DETECTIVES HAD RECEIVED the call about the fire and the body, Maura James was starting to panic. It was 9:30 a.m. in New Jersey and she had just arrived at the Delta airlines baggage claim at Newark Liberty International Airport—forty-five minutes late.

Once a Florida resident, Maura had only recently moved to New Jersey, and the turnpikes and parkways still confused her. She had gotten a late start from home, only to become lost on the way to the airport. By the time she'd gotten there, her daughter Melissa was nowhere to be found.

Maura tried her daughter's cell phone, but got no answer. She asked a man at the Delta counter if the flight—Vegas to Atlanta to Newark—had arrived or if it had been delayed. He told her that it had arrived on time and all the baggage had been claimed.

She asked if there was a Melissa James on board. He checked the computer. He said a Melissa James had been ticketed, but she'd never boarded the flight—not in Atlanta, and not in Las Vegas before that.

Maura James didn't know whether to be angry or afraid. Her daughter had irritated her before, failing to call when she said she would, but had never done anything as serious as miss a flight and not call or text-message her.

She called her daughter again and left a message.

"Melissa," she told the voice mail, "call me."

This was not how the trip had been planned. Just the day before, on Tuesday, December 13, Melissa had sent her mother a text message at 11:18 a.m. from Las Vegas:

> I leave tonight. Delta. At 10:30. Get to Atlanta at 5 a.m. Leave 6:45 a.m.
>
> Get to Newark 8:42 a.m. I'll give you flight numbers before I leave.

Melissa then called her mother a half-hour later, at 11:42 a.m. Maura James was at her desk at a construction site job in the Bristol-Myers building when her cell phone rang and her daughter's name popped up on caller ID.

When they spoke, her daughter seemed preoccupied. She appeared to be calling from a store or restaurant. There were noises in the background, people talking, and at one point Maura heard her daughter say to somebody with her, "What do you want to eat?"

Maura asked her daughter who she was with. Melissa didn't answer. There were more noises in the background that Maura couldn't make out, then Melissa said, "I'm getting ready to eat."

"Where are you?"

"KFC," said Melissa. "Hey, Mom," she added, sounding distracted, "I'll call you back after I eat."

Her mother started to ask her for the flight number, then instead asked how long Melissa planned to stay with her. All she had was the arrival information. She didn't see anything in the text message about a return flight.

Melissa paused.

"I don't think I'm coming back," she said, and then hung up.

Maura knew that something was wrong, again.

It had been like this for years now, ever since Melissa had met a muscular man named Craig Titus, who persuaded her to move from Florida to Los Angeles to live and work with him and his muscular wife.

The couple were professional athletes, Craig a bodybuilder who had modest success, Kelly a superstar in women's fitness. Melissa, who'd done modeling and acting in her hometown off Panama City, Florida, found the couple glamorous, their lifestyle exciting, and dreamed of meeting movie stars and becoming famous herself.

She first stayed with them in 2001, when they lived in the bodybuilding mecca of Venice Beach, California, but fame and stardom didn't come as easily as she had hoped and soon Melissa was back in Panama City.

She didn't stay long, reuniting with the couple when they moved to Florida a year later. Again, it didn't work out, and back to Florida she went. Several times this went on, and each time it ended in disappointment and frustration, Melissa's plans to finish college and get on with a career forever being put on hold.

The latest time came in October 2005, when the couple—now nearing retirement from sports—recruited her to help run a store they were opening that sold fitness apparel. Called Ice Gear, the store was to open in December 2005, just days from when Melissa had called her mother and said she wasn't going to return to Las Vegas.

Maura James didn't know what the problem was this time. Melissa had complained about how the couple used to argue bitterly, especially when they were training, making Melissa—who usually lived with them, helping out with their various business enterprises—feel uncomfortable.

Vegas had also treated Melissa badly. Maura noticed that her daughter had lost weight and was stretched financially. She didn't pry into her problems.

Whatever the reason, Melissa would tell her mother when she got to New Jersey. They had always been close. Maura was willing to wait.

Yet now Melissa had not arrived. Maura called her daughter again, and got only voice mail.

IT WAS 10:24 A.M. WHEN ROBERT WILSON AND THE two other detectives, Ken Hardy and Cliff Mogg, arrived at the two-story stucco home on Adobe Arch Road, a cul-de-sac of like-looking houses about a block away from Tropicana.

When Wilson knocked on the wooden door, a brown-haired, 30ish woman with deeply tanned skin and a powerful, athletic build appeared. Wilson identified himself, then asked her for her name.

She said Kelly Ryan. The detective did a double take. Later he said he was "puzzled" and "kind of surprised." He had thought Kelly Ryan was dead in the desert.

Composing himself, Wilson explained why the detectives were there: Kelly's Jaguar had been found burning in the desert with a body in the trunk.

She reacted with shock, saying, "Oh my God!"

"Can we come in and talk to you about it?" asked Wilson.

She let them into the house. It was a home like so many in Las Vegas, spacious, new and fresh, with all the latest, from flooring to appliances—and a fraction of the cost of a similar home in LA, which had been sending so many new residents to Las Vegas.

As Kelly led the detectives through the entryway, Wilson asked if there was anybody else in the house. She said her husband had been there that morning, and then a bald, muscular man with a powerful jaw emerged on the second-floor balcony and walked down the stairs.

When he reached the detectives, he identified himself as Craig Titus. He was even more impressive up close, with bulging biceps, massive forearms, hulking shoulders and barrel chest. Together, the couple were physical specimens.

The detectives asked if the couple would speak to them about the burning Jaguar. They readily agreed, with Kelly heading off to the kitchen with Detective Robert Wilson while Craig went to the living room with Detective Mogg.

Given permission by the couple to look around the house, Detective Hardy poked around the downstairs area, including the living room and what appeared to be a bedroom off the hall that led to a laundry room and the three-car garage.

Although interviewed separately, both on tape, Craig and Kelly gave similar theories of why Kelly's Jaguar had ended up on fire with a body inside.

The night before, Kelly and Craig said, they had entertained friends—Kelly's best friend, Megan, and Megan's boyfriend—until 2 a.m., watching a movie on the big-screen TV upstairs, listening to music and talking. After the friends had left, Craig stayed up longer and Kelly went to bed.

Always an early riser, Kelly said she'd gotten up at her usual 5 a.m. to go to the bathroom and walk the dog. As she got ready to leave, she went into the laundry room to wash a load of clothes and noticed a glow coming through the door to the garage. It was her posing lights, which she shined on herself to strike practice poses for competition. Kelly explained she was a professional fitness competitor, her husband a professional bodybuilder.

Kelly said that she'd gone into the garage to turn off the lights. That's when she saw that her Jaguar was missing.

Immediately, she believed that it had been stolen by somebody they knew, and she now feared and believed the body in the truck was Melissa.

In his interview, Craig said the same thing.

The body was probably that of Melissa James.

It was the first time police had heard her name.

Asked what she had been wearing the last time they saw her, they said she'd had on blue jeans and a blue long-sleeved shirt, and that her hair had recently been dyed to a reddish-brown. Detective Mogg called Detective O'Kelley at the scene. That was the same clothing and hair color found on the corpse. A records search also found that Melissa James was a white female, 5-foot-5, 120 pounds, which matched the victim.

The couple explained that Melissa was a longtime friend they had met in Florida and was now an employee who had been living with them since October in a downstairs guest room, handling their financial matters and helping them start a clothing store. They paid her in room, board and expense money, but no salary, until the store opened.

In recent weeks, they said, they had begun to suspect that Melissa was stealing from them. New credit cards they hadn't applied for started showing up in the mail. ATM charges for items the couple hadn't bought began to register on their statement. Other financial irregularities cropped up. The couple had entrusted Melissa with their private financial information, including PINs, and now suspected she had violated that trust.

In what way? Detective Wilson asked Kelly as they sat in the kitchen.

"OK, one example, she went online and changed my pass codes," Kelly said, according to the *Las Vegas Review-Journal*, which printed excerpts from the interview. "She requested new security information be sent to her and new banking cards sent to her."

At the same time, Melissa's behavior had deteriorated. Kelly said that she'd appeared ungrateful and begun to act like she expected them to take care of her. Kelly began to fear Melissa would hurt them. Kelly had seen some powdery material in their drinking glasses and thought it was poison put there by Melissa.

Kelly told Detective Wilson that she'd confronted Melissa, giving her a letter that detailed all of the alleged misdeeds. This led to an argument, and life on Adobe Arch Road became so tense that Melissa had to move out, checking into a room at La Quinta Inn & Suites on the corner of Fort Apache and Sahara, about five miles away. Kelly was a little uncertain of the exact night she was there, saying just a night or two earlier.

The cooling-off night didn't work, and by the next day Melissa was back at the couple's home, getting into another argument about the finances. The most recent spat was just the afternoon or evening before, on Tuesday, December 13, Kelly said.

Meanwhile, Craig had purchased airline tickets for Melissa to travel back East that night—Kelly didn't have the details, but thought Melissa was going to a small town in Florida. The flight was to leave around 10 p.m.

Tensions ran high as Melissa packed. Kelly tried to help her, but Melissa was so upset she threw her things into the suitcase, while Kelly kept trying to fold them neatly, Kelly told the detective.

Kelly and Craig discussed who would take her to the

airport and which car to use. They settled on Kelly driving the Jaguar. Kelly said she and Melissa left at about 3:25 p.m., but they never arrived at the airport, getting only as far as a mini-mart called the Green Valley Grocery at the corner of Fort Apache and Hacienda, just around the corner from the couple's home.

Melissa demanded to be dropped off there. Kelly obliged. Kelly was so tired of the problems with Melissa that she didn't ask why she wanted to be dropped off, or why she had wanted to go to the airport so early.

That was the last time that Kelly saw Melissa, she said.

Kelly said she turned around and drove a quarter-mile home, where she stayed the rest of the day. At some point, Craig left in the truck to run errands.

Detective Wilson asked Kelly why the couple thought Melissa was stealing from them. She only had guesses. She mentioned that Melissa was involved in drugs with a man who had once threatened to kill her. The couple had recently found drug paraphernalia in Melissa's room, which they threw away. Kelly couldn't remember the name of the man for certain.

That was it. When pressed, she said she had no firm idea what had happened to Melissa or to the Jaguar, only that she was suspecting that Melissa's troubles were to blame. The car keys were kept in a basket at the foot of the stairs, and now they were missing. She said they had a house alarm, but that it wasn't set when the car disappeared.

"I'm fanatical about locking the doors," Kelly added. "I always lock the doors."

Asked if she ever reported any of this to police—the suspected theft, the drugs, the missing car—Kelly said she had not.

During the interviews, Detective Mogg searched Melissa's room, which was a mess: the bed unmade, clothes strewn about, items piled on the floor and on the bed. A small metal strongbox appeared to have been forced open with papers still inside. And sitting on a chair, as if placed there, was Kelly's credit card.

The detective also found numerous syringes, bloody tissues and about a dozen bottles of prescription medication.

Where, the detective asked Kelly, did she think Melissa had gone?

"I don't know," Kelly stammered. "Maybe Wal-Mart?"

The detective pressed on, asking Kelly if, when they suspected Melissa had driven off with her Jaguar, they'd called any of her friends or relatives to see if she was with them.

Kelly said she hadn't, but added that Craig had gone out looking for Melissa.

The detective asked if Craig had recruited anybody to help him.

Yes, said Kelly, he'd called a friend named Anthony Gross, whom she described as somebody Craig felt he could rely upon.

"I have his phone number in my cell phone," Kelly said. "Do you want it now?"

Detective Wilson told her he'd get it before the other detectives left.

• • •

AS KELLY SPOKE IN THE KITCHEN, DETECTIVE CLIFF Mogg was conducting his interview in the living room with Craig Titus.

Craig's account matched that of his wife, relating his concerns about Melissa's drug problem and suspicions she was stealing from them. He said she might have been committing identity theft.

Craig had additional details about Melissa's stay at the motel. He said he'd driven her to the hotel in the Jaguar the night of December 12 and checked her in late at night. He said he'd stayed with her for a couple of hours, returning home the morning of December 13—just the day before.

Craig gave a rosier view of the household situation than Kelly did, saying that when Melissa returned the day before, tensions had eased. In fact, Craig suggested that although both he and his wife had issues with Melissa, it was Kelly who had the most problems with her. He said that the two women had spoken the previous afternoon and smoothed things over, with Kelly driving Melissa to the airport at about 3 p.m. the day before, but dropping her off at the grocery store a quarter mile away. He said she'd driven the truck, not the Jaguar, as Kelly had indicated.

After Kelly returned, Craig said, they ransacked Melissa's room, finding mortgage papers for an investment house he rented out, a number of other financial documents, including tax papers, as well as an ampoule of morphine, methamphetamine and several bloody needles.

He said that later that night, about 12:30 or 1 a.m.,

he and Kelly had been worried that Melissa never made her flight. He said that he'd driven his truck to the Palace Station, a casino frequented by locals, looking for a man whom Craig described as a methamphetamine dealer Melissa knew. Craig thought Eddie may have pressured Melissa into stealing from Craig and Kelly.

"He's real cool, drug dealer, you know, 'Pay me, I'll kill ya' type, [expletive] idiot," Titus told detectives, according to the *Review-Journal*.

He added: "I'll tell ya something right now, if I find this [expletive] guy before you guys do, I'm gonna [expletive] him up. I'll call you when I do."

Craig told the detective that he and Kelly had searched the casino parking lot for Eddie's black Jeep Cherokee, but didn't find it.

When they returned home, the Jaguar was still in the garage, Craig said. Craig didn't mention the late-night visit by friends. Instead, he said that after returning from the Palace Station, he and Kelly had sat up in the bedroom, talked and watched TV. He said he'd also attended to paperwork in the office.

Asked for his theory of what had happened, Craig said he guessed that at some point Melissa had come home, disabled the house alarm and driven off in the Jaguar. As Craig spoke, Detective Mogg noticed that the house alarm was on—it was now around 1 p.m. on Thursday.

During the interview the alarm would beep, and each time Craig would turn his head in the direction of the noise. It was one of two nervous tics. The other: Craig would start clicking his lighter during pointed questions, then stop clicking it when the queries were more mundane.

The detective asked Craig about the now-operating alarm system, and he suggested that Melissa may have reset the alarm after pulling out of the driveway.

When the Jaguar had gone missing, Craig said he didn't call Melissa, but did send her a text message reading, "Where the fuck's my car?"

The outgoing message was still on Craig's cell phone, time stamped at 4:28 a.m. He showed it to Detective Mogg.

As Craig spoke about Melissa—the hour or two that he'd spent with her at the motel, the tension between her and Kelly—the detective pressed harder on the nature of the relationship. Craig acknowledged that more was going on than just work.

He and Melissa had been having an affair, and his wife didn't know.

AS MAURA JAMES STOOD AT THE AIRPORT, THINKING of how she would try to track down her missing daughter, it occurred to her that of all the phone numbers programmed into her cell phone, none belonged to the people who had been such a large part of Melissa's life, Craig Titus and Kelly Ryan. Maybe they knew what had happened to her daughter.

But how to reach them? All she knew was that about two years earlier she had written down Craig Titus' phone number—for some reason Melissa had given it to her—and thought she had left it in her desk. Maura drove home and searched the desk. To her relief, she found it in a drawer.

She dialed and got Craig's recorded message on his cell number. Maura went to work and called Craig several more times that day, leaving messages, but never getting a call back.

Maura didn't panic, yet. She told herself it was too early to call the police. At work, she looked up the names and phone numbers of Las Vegas hospitals on her computer. She called them, one by one, asking if a Melissa James had been admitted. None had anybody by that name.

As the day wore on, Maura told herself that if she didn't hear from Melissa, or from Craig or Kelly by that night, she would call the police.

It was when she got home from work that she got the phone call from her ex-husband Dennis, saying that a woman from the coroner's office in Las Vegas had called asking him if he had a daughter named Melissa James. He told her that he did, but he wasn't aware that she was in Vegas. He told the coroner's assistant that Maura would have more information and that he would pass on the number to her.

Maura told Dennis that Melissa had in fact returned to Vegas, just eight weeks earlier in October, and that she was supposed to have arrived in New Jersey just that day to spend time with her for Christmas, but never made her flight.

Maura then made the most difficult phone call of her life. The woman who answered at the coroner's office was pleasant and professional.

"Is your daughter in Las Vegas?" the woman answered.

Maura told her that she had been.

The woman asked for a description. Maura said that Melissa was slim, about 5-foot-3, with brown hair, blue eyes, pierced ears and a pair of ballet dancers tattooed on her lower back, a memory from Melissa's days as a dance student and later as the operator of her dance studio.

When Maura asked what was going on, the coroner's assistant said that a body had been found in the desert. She said nothing of the circumstances—only that it was a body.

"I'm not saying this is her," the woman said, but Maura didn't hear the rest. The room began spinning. She tried to regain control, telling herself this wasn't happening, that it was all a bad dream.

THAT NIGHT, IN LAS VEGAS, THE DETECTIVES ASsessed the case. They had tape-recorded the interviews with Craig Titus and Kelly Ryan, they had searched the house and found the drug material in Melissa's room, and they had the phone number of Anthony Gross.

Although a woman living in their home had turned up dead in their burning car, the couple were not arrested and not questioned further. There was more to do and learn.

For one, the detectives had no positive identification on the body. The couple seemed certain the victim was Melissa—but a slim doubt remained.

Investigators also needed to confirm the couple's story, starting by interviewing the friends who'd been with them the night before, plus this friend Anthony who'd helped Craig look for Melissa. They needed to track down these associates of Melissa's—Ben and

Eddie, if they were indeed two people, or different names of the same man.

Mostly, they needed to know just whom they were dealing with.

Craig Titus and Kelly Ryan, though living in a lovely house in a nice neighborhood, and though cooperative and seemingly open with investigators, might still be holding back. There were minor discrepancies in their stories—Kelly said she'd driven Melissa to the mini-mart in the Jaguar, while Craig said she'd used the truck—and certain remarks didn't add up, including Kelly's peculiar suggestion that Melissa had stolen the car to go to Wal-Mart, and Craig's seeming nervousness about the alarm system.

More critically, detectives got a hint of a motive when Craig had mentioned the affair with the apparent victim—while Kelly had said nothing about it. There was certainly tension in the house in the hours leading up to the car fire. Was the affair the cause of that?

They called themselves athletes and business people, and a quick Google search could confirm it. They were good-looking, physically fit and successful, celebrities even.

But who really, investigators needed to know, were Craig Titus and Kelly Ryan?

CHAPTER TWO

THIS WAS GOING TO BE HIS NIGHT. A CROWD OF more than 2,000 packed the Auditorium Theater in Denver on July 8, 1995, escaping an unusual Rocky Mountain heat wave that had pushed temperatures into the 90s.

At age 30, Craig Titus was hardly a kid. But the Houston-based bodybuilder had risen through the amateur ranks to become a star. With a mop of blond hair and a handsome face with a confident, cocky smile, Craig Titus stood out in a sport dominated by men whose mugs didn't live up to their bodies.

Now he had reached his biggest test: the National Physique Committee USA event. Entered as a heavyweight, Titus piled muscle upon muscle on his 5-foot-8 frame, his skin so tight it accentuated every ripple and curve, his complexion a perfect brown from spray-on tan.

"Craig was a guy that was on his way up," recalled Shawn Ray, one of the sport's most successful pro bodybuilders, who that night was doing commentary for ESPN. "He had a good look. There are not a whole lot of good-looking body builders; a lot of them were very rugged and scary-looking. Craig didn't cross that line of being non-attainable. He was a guy that, if you're on the beach and you saw him you'd say 'No wonder he's got all the hot chicks around him.' "

A victory on the NPC USA stage promised more than just a trophy and a wild ovation from the muscle-heads in the crowd.

It would earn him the golden ticket of bodybuilding: a professional card, allowing him to earn a living off of his body.

The salary would pale compared to other sports—low six figures if he was lucky—but a pro card would allow him to dedicate himself full-time to the sport, earning money by endorsing nutritional supplements, guest-posing at events and scoring a promotional contract with one of the bodybuilding magazines. He'd become a player in what the insiders called "The Industry."

Some of those same magazines had predicted Titus would capture the NPC USAs, and his confidence—never lacking—soared. And so on that Saturday evening in Denver, Craig walked onto the stage in his G-string–like posing trunks and did what bodybuilders do for the judges: flexed, strained, contorted and grunted, anything to expand their muscle mass to grotesquely huge dimensions.

When the competitors finished their poses, the judges compiled their scores, which were submitted to the master of ceremonies, Lonnie Teper, a legendary multi-hyphenate in The Industry—physical education instructor at Pasadena City College, columnist for *Muscular Development*, show promoter and, on this night, emcee for one of hundreds of shows in his career.

With the crowd anxiously awaiting the winner, Teper went through each weight class, the bantamweights, the middleweights, announcing the winners, hearing the applause, watching the competitors take their prizes, before finally making the announcement everybody was waiting for.

"Let's bring on your heavyweights!" Teper said, and the crowd cheered.

Though the criteria for evaluating one bodybuilder against another are notoriously vague—and rumors constantly swirl that judges are beholden to one faction or another in the industry—it was clear to the screeching audience in the Denver auditorium that Craig was their favorite.

TV analyst Shawn Ray's personal scorecard had Craig winning the heavyweight competition, which would give him the overall title. Although close, Ray believed Craig had a better taper—that V-shape from shoulder to waist—and leaner build than his closest competition, Phil Hernon, who appeared blockier with a bigger waist and less muscle definition.

Lonnie Teper looked at his heavyweight card and winced.

"And in second place," he announced, "Craig Titus."

There was a smattering of boos, some cheers.

Craig was stunned—then outraged. By losing the heavyweight division to Hernon, he had no shot at the overall title—or his scorecard. With angry eyes—Teper would later say he "looked like Charles Manson"—Craig ripped his competition number off his little shorts, threw it on the ground and stomped off stage.

Backstage, Craig's rampage intensified. Tears streaming down his face, he took out his anger on the furniture behind the curtain and threw away his second-place trophy.

The reaction was almost unprecedented. Bodybuilding, for all its raging testosterone—natural and artificial—is a peculiarly genteel sport, with the governing authorities imposing stiff fines and penalties for the slightest lapses in competition decorum.

To self-destruct the way Craig Titus did was unheard of, and the penalty was appropriately severe: The NPC suspended him for six months for unsportsmanlike conduct.

Hours later, Craig simmered in the hotel restaurant.

When Teper came in for a meal, Craig confronted him.

"You," Craig said, "are the reason I lost."

The middle-aged emcee, who often makes fun of his soft physique and receding hairline during his onstage banter, wondered for a moment if this 200-plus-pound monster of mass was going to kill him.

To his relief, Teper got hit by no more than Craig's words. The bodybuilder accused Teper of spreading lies and rumors about him, poisoning the judges' assessment of his abilities.

Craig stomped off, his anger boiling for months.

Little known at the time, the fair-haired fresh face of bodybuilding had reasons to be tense, and not just because he'd lost.

Titus was engaged in one of the ugliest fights of his life, and by year's end he'd have much more to worry about than a fine. For Craig Titus was on his way to becoming one of the sport's most infamous figures, attracting the title "the Bad Boy of Bodybuilding."

IT WASN'T ALWAYS LIKE THAT.

He started out small, literally. Born on January 14, 1965, to Michael Titus, who dug tunnels for a living, and homemaker Sandra Fulmer Titus, Craig Titus was a short, puny, 5-foot-6, 130-pound junior at Riverview High School in Michigan.

He competed on the wrestling squad, in a lighter-weight division. Although he would later claim to have made it as a state wrestling champ—later in life, Craig would come to overstate his exploits and understate his age—the official records say otherwise; no Craig Titus ever so much as made it to the finals, much less won them, according to the Michigan High School Athletic Association.

But what he may have lacked on the mat, he made up for in the weight room. Craig spent countless hours in the gym, impressing his wrestling coach with his dedication and drive. It was a labor of love, Craig discovering the pump high that has addicted generations of bodybuilders. He found his future.

"I would sit and read the muscle magazines," Craig once told an interviewer, "looking at and admiring athletes like Mike Christian, Robby Robinson and Lee Labrada. I was amazed at how awesome they looked. I knew I wanted to become a bodybuilder."

The trio of Christian, Robinson and Labrada were among a dozen or so competitors who dominated the industry in the late 1970s and 1980s, when bodybuilding was in transition, still trying to find its place after the sport lost its favorite son, an Austrian immigrant named Arnold Schwarzenegger, to Hollywood after collecting a string of Mr. Olympia titles.

The charismatic Schwarzenegger had introduced bodybuilding to a mainstream audience with the help of the popular book and documentary *Pumping Iron*, which mythologized Gold's Gym and Venice Beach, and made the niche sport something approaching sexy and cool. Nobody could fill the vacuum left by Arnold's retirement, and not even a temporary return to competition could bring the sport back to its late 70s popularity.

Still, when Craig Titus toiled in the high school gym, bodybuilding held all the allure that it always did. He would add his name to the sport's long history.

ALTHOUGH THE PARAGON OF MALE PERFECTION IS personified by ancient Greek athletes chisled in marble, the actual practice of what people now call bodybuilding—the sculpting of the body for the sake of aesthetics, rather than to prepare it for a sport or battle—didn't emerge until well into the 19th century.

The father of bodybuilding was a German named Eugen Sandow, who turned his gymnast's body into sheer bulk by lifting a bar with bells at each end filled with shot or sand. Sandow grew big at just the same time as photography did, and soon popular postcards obliterated Victorian discretion by featuring photos of the mustachioed German with rippling abs, bulging biceps and protruding veins, wearing only an imitation fig leaf while standing on a dead animal pelt.

America, particularly, liked looking at muscular men. Vaudeville showman Flo Ziegfeld promoted Sandow as "The World's Most Perfectly Developed Man" and Sandow parlayed his fame by publishing *Physical Culture* magazine, sparking a run on the sales of dumbbells and barbells.

Never shy about flaunting his masculinity, legend had it that Sandow suffered an ironic fate. According to Schwarzenegger's *The New Encyclopedia of Modern Bodybuilding*, Sandow was said to have died of a brain hemorrhage in 1925 when he tried to single-handedly haul his car out of a ditch after it ran off the road.

By the time of Sandow's allegedly fatal flash of machismo, however, bodybuilding had taken hold of Europe and America, with Sandow's early notoriety paving the way for another icon, an American named Bernarr Macfadden, who sponsored the first major competition, the contest for "the Most Perfectly Developed Man in America," held in Madison Square Garden in 1903. The winner got the then-handsome sum of $1,000.

In 1921, the prize went to an Italian immigrant named Angelo Siciliano, who later sold mail-order "dynamic tension" workout regimes under his new name, Charles Atlas. The ads in boys' and men's magazines, featuring a cartoon of a skinny kid getting darned tired of having sand kicked in his face at the beach by a bigger guy, ran for some fifty years, well into the childhood of an undersized Michigan kid named Craig Titus.

The 1970s were the glory days of the sport, as bodybuilding moved from Muscle Beach in Santa Monica to Venice Beach a few miles south, and into the public's consciousness. A former bodybuilding competitor named Joe Weider had brought rival bodybuilding factions into his immensely successful Mr. Olympia contests sponsored by the Weider-run International Federation of Bodybuilding and promoted in Weider-owned magazines like *Flex* and *Muscle & Fitness*, to form a bodybuilding empire that exists to this day.

The same conglomeration took place in the amateur ranks. By the 1980s, the National Physique Committee broke with the once-dominant American Athletic Union to become the premiere amateur organization, and the only one—for men, and later, women—to feed winners into the pro ranks of the IFBB.

At its core, bodybuilding, for those who practiced it or watched its icons, symbolized a state of endless sex and high self-esteem, best summed up by Schwarzenegger, who famously said in 1979, "Having a pump is like having sex. I train two, sometimes three times a day. Each time I get a pump. It's great. I feel like I'm coming all day."

Nearly twenty years later, nothing had changed.

As Craig Titus and the other competitors strutted onto the Denver stage in 1995, his appeal to women rippled like his muscles, and the crowd—mostly men—cheered as much out of envy as respect for his build.

"There are women out there who just flock to these guys," says Ron Avidan, who runs the leading bodybuilding website, Getbig.com, the clearinghouse for news and gossip. "I've personally seen it. You know, it's just absolutely amazing. It really blows my mind. I went to a party with some bodybuilders, and these women would just fling themselves at them. I mean, if you're a player, you can have a girl every night. There was no shortage of women for these guys."

There had always been a gay element in bodybuilding, and the very sight of thousands of men cheering beefy guys in tiny briefs raises certain questions. Still, those in the industry insist that it's dominated by confirmed heterosexuals, who will only switch sides if the money's right.

"They don't do 'gay videos,'" Avidan chuckles. "They do 'posing videos.' A lot of them used to be strippers. They're not gay, they're just stripping. Good money, you know."

Although Southern California is ground zero for bodybuilding, competitors are scattered throughout the United States and overseas. And while they seem to be raging narcissists subsisting on crowd approval of their bodies, their lives are spent mostly alone, a man and his barbells, sweating it out for hours on end in a gym, meeting his buff brethren only at the handful of competitions throughout the year: the USAs, the Arnold Classic, the Iron Man and the grand-daddy of them all, the Olympia.

In the earlier days, they got the latest dirt on who was hot and who was not, as well as the behind-the-scenes info, in the magazine columns or on 900 numbers that posted the latest updates for $1.99 a minute. By the 1990s, the Internet changed everything, with its reach and promise of anonymity, so that now bodybuilders spend nearly as much time behind a keyboard as they do in the gym, chattering like MySpace-obsessed teenagers on message boards.

Ron Avidan's Getbig.com site, operated out of his Los Angeles home, leads the pack. Employed by day at a San Fernando Valley company that distributes nutritional supplements, the Israeli-born, Los Angeles–raised Avidan, tall, with thick glasses, acknowledges, "I'm not a bodybuilder, I haven't been a bodybuilder and I don't intend to be a bodybuilder. I'm a fan of bodybuilding. So I started Getbig in 1995, intended as a place where people can get information on bodybuilding."

Getbig.com features photos of bulging bodybuilders from pro and amateur sites, the results of the major contests, interviews that Avidan conducts with the leading figures in the industry and, most popular of all, a message board that serves as the leading forum of communication between competitors and fans. Designed for an almost exclusively male audience, the board is a clearinghouse not only of news and information, but of griping, catty remarks and disinformation.

"Most of the people who post on this website are morons," says Lonnie Teper, who then admits he spends hours each week on the site. "They can't wait to trash you or write bad things. They have no life other than sitting on there all day long. There was always somebody dying who wasn't dying, sick who wasn't sick."

Operated in his off hours at no profit to maintain his independence from the ruling bodies, magazines and supplement companies that power bodybuilding, Avidan scrambles to keep the site current, traveling the country to competitions, taking many of the pictures himself, and transcribing his taped interviews, often late at night after work. After its launch, the site became so popular that his original server kept crashing and he had to upgrade. And among the leading sources of news and gossip on Getbig was Craig Titus, whose career took off at about the same time as the website.

"You can be the best bodybuilder in the world, but if you're not in the top ten, you need to have something else there," says Avidan. "For me, it's entertainment value. I see a bodybuilder who's great, but doesn't say anything, it's OK. But if they say a few words, if they give you something to talk about, for good or for bad, then you've got something else. And Craig was not one to stop talking."

Over the course of his career, Craig Titus gave several interviews to Ron Avidan, some in which he spoke at length about his highs and lows—often the lows. Avidan was among the few who never seriously clashed with Craig, and they remained, if not friends, certainly friendly up until the end. Among the last people Craig talked to, when his world was about to come crashing down, was Ron Avidan.

"His physique was OK," says Avidan. "He didn't have a great physique. He wasn't one of the best bodybuilders. It was his attitude and his style and his talk that made him considered one of the bad boys of bodybuilding. He would be right up in your face."

In person, Craig, like many bodybuilders, is shorter than one might imagine. After high school, he topped out at 5-foot-8, diminutive by the standards of any other sport but horse racing, but ideal for bodybuilding. Some of the sport's most famous figures measure well south of 6 feet, no matter what their padded résumés say.

Shawn Ray, who claims to stand 5-foot-7, but seems an inch shy of that, enjoyed a storied eighteen-year bodybuilding career, winning nearly every award except the Olympia, and now enjoys a comfortable retirement with a beautiful wife, cute baby, investment properties, endorsement contracts and a Mercedes with a personalized license plate.

A short frame serves as the perfect armature for sculpting muscles, the mass compressed and more impressive looking; on a taller man the muscles become elongated and lack that critical definition that the judges and muscle-heads desire.

AFTER HIGH SCHOOL, CRAIG TITUS HAD A GROWTH spurt, adding two inches in height, dozens of pounds in weight, made hard by his diligent iron-pumping. He bypassed college to labor in a Houston gym to shape and build his body in the late 1980s, all without pay.

The bodybuilding industry lacks signing bonuses or minor leagues or the Olympic loopholes that allow supposed amateur swimmers and track stars to make money on the side. Amateur means amateur, and while pursuing his dreams of bodybuilding glory, Titus held down a regular job.

"I actually worked with my father for about six years right after high school building tunnels: storm drains, subways, sewage systems, hundreds of feet under the face of the earth," he once told Avidan in an interview posted on Getbig.com. "It was real scary. I saw of couple of gentlemen lose their lives. I saw my father almost die, as he got hit in the face with a four-inch-high beam, and his jaw cracked wide open. I saw some scary things. I broke almost every finger in my hands."

Craig claimed he and his father even set a world record in 1993. "We mined one hundred and one feet in an eight-hour shift," he said.

Whether that was true is impossible to confirm—Guinness doesn't keep tunneling records. He never spoke much about his early years in Houston, years marked by love, then heartbreak.

Harris County, Texas, wedding records show that on August 30, 1985, he married Susan Kathleen Bell in a speck of a town called Cee Vee. Susan was six years older than Craig, 26 to his 20. Craig rarely talked about Susan over the years except to criticize her, and the details of this union are fuzzy.

According to Texas birth records, three years after they married, Susan gave birth on July 11, 1988, to twins, a boy they named Aaron Colby Titus and a girl, Ashley Marie Titus.

What joy these children brought ended quickly and horribly, as just six months later, on January 3, 1989, Aaron died.

The official cause of death remains locked in Texas records unavailable to the public. In interviews, Craig said his son died of sudden infant death syndrome, and the loss weighed heavily on him in times good and bad. He said he always wore a gold necklace with the symbol of the Egyptian god of power on it "just so I never forget him. The necklace has been around my neck since his death, and I wear it all the time. I have it on right now. My father gave it to me the day my son was buried. My father was living in Cairo, Egypt, at the time, and he brought it to me saying that 'This will give you the strength needed to get through this.' "

Around the time of Aaron's death, the Tituses separated: what role the tragedy had can only be speculated. After four years of marriage, their divorce was finalized on July 31, 1989, according to Harris County records. Susan was 30 and Craig was 24.

By now, Craig was deeply committed to bodybuilding, spending time in the gym when he wasn't digging tunnels. His workout regimen put him at a tight 180 pounds of pure muscle, well-defined, if not necessarily huge by the standards of the sport, which by the late 1970s and early 80s was dominated by man-beasts whose bizarrely outsized muscles made Charles Atlas appear as skimpy as the boy in his cartoons.

In 1988, Craig Titus entered his first important event, the Houston Bodybuilding Championship, an amateur competition. Registered as a middleweight, he won not only his class, but the overall title despite his lean build. The victory was a turning point.

"I was hooked," he told the bodybulding website MuscleNet.com. Craig now was a disciple not only of the weight room, but of the strict dietary practices of world-class bodybuilders. He followed his heroes in eating numerous small meals a day, spreading out the calories, while shunning carbohydrates and focusing on lots of protein.

It's a diet that leaves a body perpetually hungry and

the disposition nasty. Bodybuilders in the days before competition are so hungry they can't sleep through the night and the high vegetable diet makes them gassy. They are, on competition days, foul of temper and of odor.

"You're eating small meals every two-and-a-half hours, because you want to keep your blood sugar levels high," says Lonnie Teper. "Imagine a fireplace. How do you keep the flames up? You're throwing in the wood—and this is your food. The flames go up, and they go down, and then you've got to feed it more food again. Down and up, down and up. And when you're down, you're starving. You're actually starving, because you're getting so little caloric intake. You may be at three hundred calories a meal, and those are the longest two to two-and-a-half hours you've ever had."

Craig embraced all of it.

The next year, he took the overall titles at the 1989 NPC Houston Bodybuilding Championships, competing again as a middleweight, and in 1990, Craig traveled to California to compete on a bigger stage, in the ESPN-sponsored Tournament of Champions at a high school in Fontana. Now entered as a heavyweight, he finished third, boosting his confidence when he returned to Texas.

Teper's first memory of the then up-and-comer was of meeting him in December 1990.

"I was visiting a friend who lived in Houston and he was telling me about this new kid on the block named Craig Titus," he recalls. "He said, 'This guy's going to be a pro. He's awesome.' He introduced me to Craig Titus in the gym. Craig said, 'I met you before. You emceed a show called Tournament of Champions. I finished third.' Well, I didn't remember that. Anyway, we talked, and I watched him work out. He was a good-looking kid, very polite, very courteous. I said to my friend, 'I can see what you're talking about. This guy has great potential.' "

At the time, Craig had beefed up to 205 pounds—"small, but ripped," according to Teper—with near-perfect muscle definition. It was a look that he would never maintain. As he gained mass, he lost some definition and had trouble keeping his stomach stuck in. Many observers said Craig was never as impressive later in his career as he was as a young amateur.

Several months after chatting with Teper, in early 1992, Titus traveled to Los Angeles to compete in another regional competition called the NPC Ironman/Ironmaiden. This time Teper took notice—as did everybody else—and Craig took the overall title.

"The Ironman/Ironmaiden was a pretty big regional show where people would come from out of state to do it because they wanted to get the attention of the writers and the photographers," recalled Ron Harris, a bodybuilder and journalist who at the time was working with a producer who packaged shows for ESPN. "We had sort of known about Craig already because we had scouts all over the country. So we shot the show for the contest highlights on the program, and then the next day we went to Gold's Gym in Fullerton and shot a profile, interview and training footage of him."

Like most who first encountered Craig, Ron Harris was struck as much by his charm and looks as he was by his physique. "He had the blond hair, the blue eyes.

He was a really handsome guy and we were all about putting marketable-looking people on the show," said Harris. "He also had a really good physique; those two qualities just don't often inhabit the same individual."

With these amateur notches under his belt, Craig was now poised to become a professional. Under the tough rules of the International Federation of Bodybuilding at the time, Craig had to finish first overall in an NPC-sanctioned national competition to get his pro card.

He trained hard in 1992, and took a trip West in 1993 to compete in the NPC USA Championships in Santa Monica.

Teper, who was emceeing the weigh-in at a Holiday Inn, saw Craig, and they exchanged hellos. Craig had a girl on his arm, one of many girlfriends over the years—"It was like musical chairs," Teper recalled.

Craig studied the competitors and said, "Man, I'm not afraid of this lineup. I can do well. I know I can hold my own in this lineup."

He did, to a point. Although he didn't get his pro card, he finished fourth against some of the world's top bodybuilders.

More important, the bodybuilding press embraced him. Although still not a pro, he scored the November 1993 cover of *MuscleMag International*. Craig wore yellow-and-blue skintight striped overalls to showcase his bulging muscles, and sported a California tan and surfer hair. A female bodybuilder in a purple thong bikini is pressing her body against his, and Craig is gripping her toned thigh.

It would be the first of dozens of magazine covers, many while Craig was still an amateur.

In June 1994, Craig returned to the USAs in New Orleans and narrowly missed getting his pro card, finishing second behind Dennis Newman, a Floridian who just ten weeks later was hospitalized with leukemia. Newman nearly died, slipping into obscurity before making a full recovery and a surprising return to bodybuilding in the late 90s.

By now Craig was a massive 270 pounds, twice his weight as a high school wrestler, and all of it muscle. He had another second-place finish that year, this time at the NPC National Championships in Orlando, Florida, to Paul DeMayo, then known as "Quadzilla" for his enormous thighs.

Craig was now a star. He later graced the cover of *Flex* magazine with the headline "Total body shocking with Craig Titus," featuring a picture of him hanging from a pull-up bar wearing only a red G-string. The story, by senior writer John Little, called Craig "the latest blond Adonis" who was "in very hard shape this contest."

"The only knock I heard," wrote Little, "was that he still possessed a thick waistline, the dimensions of which will have to be contoured slightly if he's ever to break his 'always a bridesmaid, never a bride' syndrome."

From this, Craig landed on more magazine covers and began dating one of the biggest sex symbols in women's bodybuilding, a buxom brunette *Playboy* model named Debee Halo, who appeared in the magazine's *Locker Room Fantasies* special issue and *Hard Bodies* video.

According to magazine accounts, Craig and Debee lived in the fast lane of bodybuilding, traveling to Spain and other countries and moving in together in an apartment in Marina del Rey, California, adjacent to Venice Beach, where Craig now trained at the famed Gold's Gym.

Despite his growing fame, Craig's near misses for his pro card began to grate on him. After the Nationals in Orlando, an angry Craig called Teper to criticize the winner, saying, "Why don't you put in your column that Paul DeMayo has the symmetry of a frog?"

In the hypersensitive world of bodybuilding, dissing a rival's symmetry is akin to telling your wife she has fat thighs, and Teper was reluctant to go there.

"Craig, that's pretty harsh, man," Teper replied. "I don't want to do that. Paul's a friend of mine."

Teper eventually did run quotes from Craig—minus the frog analogy: "I tempered it, and had him say, 'The guy doesn't have good symmetry.'"

The episode introduced Teper to the other side of Craig, a side that bodybuilders tended to keep quiet, but one that Craig would increasingly flaunt like his glutes at competition. For all the machismo, bodybuilding is very much like a beauty contest, mannered on the surface, catty behind the scenes. To go public with a complaint ran contrary to the tone set by the amiable and politic Arnold.

"He was probably trying to build up his confidence," Teper recalls of Craig's first attempts at trash talking. "He's probably trying to bring out to the judges, who may be reading my column, that 'This guy has crappy symmetry, why don't you notice that?' It's a combination of insecurity and ego."

For Craig, both of those personality traits collided violently within months. In 1995, he would compete in Denver as the odds-on favorite, only to go bananas at losing again. His looks got him the women and his actions gave him the bad boy rep, but few knew just how bad this boy really was.

On the day he took the stage in Denver, he was one step away from prison.

CHAPTER THREE

ON A FALL DAY IN 1995, IN A FEDERAL BUILDING IN Lafayette, Louisiana, US District Judge Rebecca Doherty called court to order. Standing before her was a muscular 30-year-old man, one of the most famous practitioners of his sport, having recently graced the covers of *Muscular Development*, *MuscleMag International* and *Iron Man*.

But on this day, his notoriety impressed no one. There was a drug war to fight, and Craig Titus was sleeping with the enemy.

In the early and mid-1990s, long before the Twin Towers toppled, the national agenda focused on drugs, not terrorists. Immense federal resources went to stop the import and distribution of narcotics, and Congress passed laws federalizing drug crimes that previously had been the domain of the states. The best way an ambitious FBI special agent in charge or local US attorney could get ink was to score a major drug bust and stage a press conference showing off the goods—along with the expensive cars, electronics and weapons seized by drug forfeiture rules.

In those days, even a relative small fry in the drug trade could attract the full attention of a special federal and local task force, and a quotable quote from an ambitious US Attorney. And in September 1994, just such an operation, made up of investigators from the Louisiana State Police Narcotics Division and agents from the Drug Enforcement Administration, was empowered to battle the flow of drugs into southern Louisiana.

It intercepted a shipment of methylenedioxymethamphetamine, more commonly known as the party drug Ecstasy, that had been express-mailed from Houston to New Iberia, 140 miles west of New Orleans.

The shipment included a Baggie containing 390 Ecstasy tablets. On that Baggie were the fingerprints of Houston resident Craig Titus.

Craig was arrested and accused of being a partner in a drug scheme with a 27-year-old resident of New Iberia named Walter Pellerin. Authorities said Pellerin had contacted Craig by pager asking first for steroids, then for Ecstasy. Authorities claimed that Craig had arranged for the shipment of Ecstasy from his home in Texas to Pellerin in Louisiana.

Craig would claim he was merely a middleman, connecting buyer with seller on one occasion, and that he didn't actually ship the pills himself. That, he claimed, was done by his then-roommate, whose name wasn't revealed in court. Craig professed not to know how his fingerprints got on the Baggie full of Ecstasy, but said he may have innocently touched the Baggies in their home.

Although authorities could never prove Craig had

mailed the drugs, they had enough evidence to squeeze him, and he capitulated, cooperating with federal authorities to help catch bigger fish. The details are sketchy, hidden in sealed court papers, but according to the documents made public, Craig said that he flew to Washington "at my own expense" to "set up a drug dealer for the government, which I did, who is now in jail."

Newly turned drug mole Craig Titus said he also traveled to Louisiana "on my own expense" to reveal more details to what he frustratingly considered nonreceptive law enforcement officials. "They have all the information to totally arrest the whole Ecstasy ring in Houston," he would complain in court, "but I guess they are not interested in doing that."

Although by all accounts he did everything authorities asked of him, Craig still faced serious drug charges. On December 13, 1994, he was indicted on charges of conspiracy to distribute Ecstasy and possession with intent to distribute Ecstasy.

Four months later, on April 17, 1995, he pleaded guilty before Judge Doherty to possession with intent to distribute the drug. The plea came "pursuant to a written plea agreement," according to legal documents, and Craig's sentencing was put off for six months.

Despite Craig's growing profile in bodybuilding, no details of his drug case made even the local newspapers in Louisiana and only rumors of his problems penetrated the bodybuilding community. Nothing appeared in print in the bodybuilding magazines, and certainly no mention was made in any of the articles linked to Craig's covers, which accentuated the positive and focused on his training and diet regimens.

What little news coverage came from the case focused instead on Pellerin, who was sentenced by Judge Doherty on June 1, 1995, to 12 months in prison, the lowest possible term under mandatory federal sentencing guidelines. A contrite Pellerin had pleaded guilty to possession with intent to distribute 950 Ecstasy tablets, according to local press accounts.

The prosecutor, Assistant US Attorney Luke Walker, who was also prosecuting Craig, said that Pellerin had cooperated with police and helped in the arrest of "another drug dealer," leading to authorities recommending the low sentence. Probation was not an option.

"Unfortunately, there are consequences to our actions, and at times those consequences are harsh. This is one of those times," Judge Doherty told Pellerin, according to a report in the local paper, the Baton Rouge *Advocate*. "But you can use it as a positive or a negative. You can let this turn you bitter and turn you into a person you would not want to know, or you can use it as a very positive thing."

Craig Titus' name did not appear in the *Advocate* news story or anywhere else in print, but that didn't stop the rumors, which intensified in July 1995 when Craig competed in Denver.

Show emcee Lonnie Teper was among those who had heard about Craig's drug problems.

"The guy in Houston, that friend who first introduced me to Craig, he was always telling me stuff. I didn't really want to get involved in that type of stuff. It's a lot of hearsay," said Teper. "He called me up the week of the USA, this guy, and says, 'I want you to hear this phone call, this DEA agent.'"

Teper told his friend he didn't want to be involved, but the friend insisted, saying, "You have to hear this."

Teper heard a click and then another person coming onto the line in a conference call, described as a DEA agent.

"Hey," Teper heard the third man ask on the phone, "what did you tell me earlier this evening?"

The purported agent answered, "Craig's going to be arrested in Denver for selling Ecstasy."

"I don't want to get involved in this," Teper recalls saying. " I don't want the sport to get hurt. I'm part of the sport. I'm not only a writer, I'm an emcee of the show, I'm friends with the promoters, I'm really good friends with Jim Manion, the NPC president. Everyone's trying to tie drugs into bodybuilding, rather than looking at all the good things it's done. It's saved people's lives. It's given them self-esteem."

Fearing the spectacle of a bodybuilder getting arrested during competition, Teper called the promoter of the show.

"This is what I've been told," Teper said to the promoter. "I have no idea if this is going to happen or not. But I know if it is true, and if they're going to try to make bodybuilding look bad, they go and arrest the guy with a search warrant when he's on stage, what a disaster for our event. Headlines."

In the end, the promoter didn't approach Craig—and Craig didn't get arrested at the show. In fact, unknown to everybody, he had already pleaded guilty and was awaiting sentencing. But it got back to Craig that Teper had spoken to the promoters and, Teper says,

"He felt that that then caused some of the judges to change their votes."

Thus the confrontation in the hotel restaurant.

What nobody could appreciate at the time was how much pressure Craig was under. If the judge later put him in a penitentiary, it could be a year or more before he would have a chance to compete again, and that's if bodybuilding—always sensitive about its image—would take him back.

"I had been going back and forth from LA to Louisiana battling my conspiracy charge," Craig later told an interviewer for MuscleNet.com. "Rumors were circulating around the contest hotel in Denver like you wouldn't believe. People were actually saying that I was going to jail for twenty years. The one that really made me mad was 'If Craig wins this show, the DEA is going to arrest him on stage.' "

In hindsight, Craig thought he could have handled it better, perhaps coming forward and revealing the truth: that he had pleaded guilty to drug charges and was facing a year, or perhaps less, in prison. But the competition consumed him. The magazines had picked him to win everything, and he had already beaten his closest competition, Phil Hernon, twice before.

So when Hernon's name was called, "I was furious," Craig acknowledged to MuscleNet.com. "I stormed off stage. I somehow felt that the rumors of jail delayed me in turning pro. After cooling down and realizing what a big mistake I made, I came to the conclusion that I lost because I simply wasn't good enough to be a pro yet."

Even that night, he had composed himself enough to realize that it was time for damage control. He invited

John Romano, a writer for *Muscular Development* magazine, into his hotel room to give him the scoop on why he'd marched off stage and what was going on with the drug case. The article was very positive, in Craig's view, and "It felt good to finally get the truth out and put an end to all the rumors."

Craig later came to terms with Teper. When he found out that Teper was merely asking promoters whether the rumors were true or not out of worry about the impact a possible arrest would have on Craig and the sport, "I felt terrible. Lonnie and I are very good friends and he is definitely an asset to the sport of bodybuilding. Getting on his bad side was not a good idea."

IN OCTOBER 1995, THREE MONTHS AFTER THE DENver show, Craig was back in Judge Doherty's courtroom in Louisiana to determine whether he would go to prison, like Pellerin, or get off with probation.

The hearing began with the judge going over a presentencing report. Along with information about Craig's income—at the time just $2,000 a month—it discussed the until-then secret details of the drug case. At issue was the exact amount of Ecstasy that Craig was accused of helping send.

This was no technicality; under federal laws at the time, a few grams' difference in weight could mean the difference between prison and probation.

Ecstasy, unlike prescription medication, is a homemade drug with no accepted standards of weights and measures; one tablet could weigh more or less than another of equal strength.

In Craig's case, some of the drugs he was charged with possessing—about 500 tablets—hadn't even been weighed by authorities, just counted. Prosecutors could only estimate the weight, based on the readings of other tablets seized in the case that were put on a scale.

To resolve the debate, a drug agent took the stand at Craig's hearing and testified that all the tablets seized seemed about the same size, but that he could only guess if the tablets Craig possessed weighed the same as the ones seized.

"All right," said Judge Doherty at the conclusion of the testimony, "Mr. Titus, this is a very close question."

"Yes, ma'am," said Craig.

"If this matter were not a homemade concoction, today you would be assessed those additional five hundred tablets. . . . If one of those tablets had been weighed, you would be looking at a very different matter here."

It was a huge break for Craig. The judge failed to find by a preponderance of evidence that the unweighed drugs should be considered for sentencing.

"Mr. Titus," she said, "you need to realize how very close you came on that one."

"I do, Your Honor," said Craig.

She then considered his punishment based on the weight of drugs the prosecution could prove Craig had helped transport. Doing the math, the judge decided that Craig should be sentenced for possessing the equivalent of 13.9 kilos of marijuana (weed laws were the baseline for Ecstasy). It made for a lighter sentence than if he'd had those extra Ecstasy tablets included, but Craig still faced prison time of a year or more.

Craig's lawyer, Gregory Thibodeaux, a local attorney being paid by the government because Craig claimed he had no money, tried to further reduce the sentence. He argued that Craig should serve less time because he was merely a "minor participant" in the drug scheme. Craig contended he had never personally mailed any drugs anywhere, that he was merely a "middleman" who'd contacted a third person, who actually sent the shipments to Louisiana.

The judge reacted skeptically.

"Despite the fact that Mr. Titus may have served as a 'middleman' in the distribution of Ecstasy, without his assistance the offense could not have been carried out," she said.

Craig's attorney disagreed, saying that, "Mr. Titus was not in Houston nor in Louisiana at the time the people were transporting Ecstasy." Thibodeaux said that Craig's role was "merely as a contact. He provided a telephone number."

The rest had been carried out by Walter Pellerin, the man sentenced months earlier, and by others, the defense lawyer said.

"I certainly understand your argument," the judge said. "But the argument you are making can also be made about the drug kingpin. A lot of times they aren't around."

With that, she refused to reduce his level of legal responsibility and thus the sentence.

"All right," she said, "does defendant have anything to say or offer in mitigation of punishment?"

Craig did. This was his opportunity to throw himself on the mercy of the court, using some of that charm that had rocketed him to the highest levels of amateur bodybuilding.

"Your Honor," he began, "I pled guilty to this because I did play a part in it, and I was accepting responsibility of it. [But] if I go to jail, my entire . . . career is ruined. I don't have a trade or job. I have a profession. If I go and serve time, it hits the magazines, my life as a bodybuilder is over with. That's all I've worked for for the last fifteen years. There is no getting out and reestablishing that."

Craig said he realized that the judge had to follow the sentencing guidelines, "but I'm just wondering if there is something else you could do besides me going to prison, some other way I can serve this punishment out. I have suffered greatly for my mistake. It's already been printed [in the magazines] and my career is hanging on a thread now."

"Mr. Titus," the judge said, "I agree with you. I think there are much more profitable ways that you can benefit society rather than going to prison. I also understand and—trust me—I truly appreciate the degree to which your career and life have been altered, and in fact, pretty much ruined. The problem is, there is nothing I can do."

Judge Doherty said the sentencing guidelines provided "very, very limited maneuvering room, and I've maneuvered in that room for you as best I can." If she gave him a lighter sentence, she said, the appeals court would simply raise it back up. She noted that she had already given him the benefit of the doubt on the total weight of the drugs.

"Unfortunately, my hands are tied," she said.

Craig reminded her that he had been working with authorities, that he had traveled on his own dime to Washington and Louisiana.

"Again, Mr. Titus, I tend to agree with you," the judge said. "It is well known by everyone involved how I feel about this substantial assistance provision, but my hands are tied on that."

The judge noted that she had spoken with the prosecutor, Luke Walker, and Craig's attorney Gregory Thibodeaux about sentencing Craig to community service, perhaps involving other weightlifters, instead of prison.

"I think that would benefit society a heck of a lot more than our paying twenty-eight thousand dollars to put you in a facility, but I don't have that option." If she did, she said, she would "probably exercise it in this case." Even that day, she had sat down with Walker and "completely reworded the guidelines" based on the anticipated testimony of the agent saying he didn't know exactly how much of the drug was involved.

"It probably upsets me almost as much as it does you, because I have a son about your age, and it seems to me a tragedy that your life is destroyed today," she said. "But I don't have any choice. I have done all I can do for you."

The judge then paused and thought for a moment.

She asked lawyers—one more time—to go over the history of the case, and Craig's role in the drug trafficking. Maybe there was something she had missed before, she said.

Prosecutor Walker again explained how the drug ring worked—how Pellerin had contacted Craig, and how the drugs had then gotten back to Pellerin. The defense attorney repeated that there was no proof that Craig actually shipped the drugs, saying that he'd merely received a page while in Virginia training and had hooked up Pellerin with a contact.

Listening to this, the judge asked Craig, "How did Mr. Pellerin know to contact you?"

Then, realizing that Craig couldn't simply answer, she said, "Do you wish to give this testimony?"

Craig replied, "I would like to answer your question, Your Honor."

After taking an oath to tell the truth and being advised by the judge to consult with his attorney before testifying, Craig not only explained his role in the Ecstasy deal, but provided details on bodybuilding's badly kept dirty little secret.

He began his testimony by saying that prior to 1994, he had visited two cities in Louisiana for a bodybuilding seminar and two guest appearances, and that Walter Pellerin was one of the promoters who'd set up the shows.

Later, Pelllerin and a woman went to Houston and visited Craig.

"I took them out to a club and . . . they were doing Ecstasy in the club," said Craig. "And they said there was a big market for it in Louisiana. At that point, nothing was done. Then at a later date, he asked me if I could get him Ecstasy. I told him I knew somebody that could."

"Why did he ask you?" the judge asked. "Someone wouldn't ask me whether or not they could get Ecstasy. Why did he think to ask you?"

"He was my guy in Louisiana that gave me steroids

for my profession," said Craig, his first public acknowledgment that his muscles came from more than pumping iron and strict dieting. "And he asked me if I could hook him up with Ecstasy in Houston because it's a well-known fact in Louisiana and everywhere else that Houston is the main manufacturer of Ecstasy."

When Pellerin met Craig in the club, he assumed that Craig would know where to get it; he was right.

"I set him up with someone who'd get him Ecstasy, and he could continue to send me Winstrol"—a synthetic anabolic steroid derived from testosterone—"so I could compete, because he knew chicken farmers in Louisiana—"

"He knew what?" the judge interrupted.

"Chicken farmers in Louisiana where he got the steroids from," said Craig. "They use steroids for chickens in Louisiana, from what I understand."

"Which argues that perhaps you ought not be messing with them, Mr. Titus."

"Yes, you are probably right," he said. "Professional bodybuilders, that's one of the things we did. And a lot of other professional athletes do it. Fortunately, at this time, I don't do it anymore, because I can't."

"You shouldn't anyway, Mr. Titus," the judge said. "It seems to me something they give chickens would be something you might not want to put in your system. Which brings up: Does your mama know that you are doing this? But that's neither here nor there."

In admitting he'd built up his body the same way farmers plump their chickens, Craig broke an unwritten rule in bodybuilding against speaking frankly about his steroid use. The sport has a peculiar approach to steroids. Everybody knows that their use is widespread—one look at the mutant bodies proves this—and almost everybody knows they aren't good for you in the long run.

And yet, professional contests didn't test for steroids, even though some did test for diuretics, used just before shows to suck the water from the fat to pull the skin as tightly as possible to the muscles. Diuretics have sent plenty of bodybuilders to the hospital, but then, steroids' effects were also well known: cramps, headaches, rashes, lethargy, gagging, vomiting, burning tongue, sore nipples, nose bleeds, hypertension, heart disease, damaged liver, acne, male breasts, depression, aggression and loss of libido.

Other sports, like track and field, bicycling and, later, baseball, have implemented some form of steroid testing. And yet pro bodybuilding has rejected it time and again. The competition was so fierce, the stakes so high, that steroids remained a fact of bodybuilding, and no "natural bodybuilder," as the steroid-free competitors call themselves, stood a chance against those on the juice.

In any event, for Craig Titus, the steroids served as his entrée into other drugs, the Ecstasy-for-chicken-steroids deal now landing him in federal court fighting for his freedom—and his career. But he insisted that he'd never personally sent any Ecstasy anywhere, except to bring it to the woman, whose name was Dawn.

"I got scared and said, 'I'm not doing it anymore,' " Craig said.

Judge Doherty still wasn't convinced of Craig's professed minor role. She asked him how his fingerprints came to be on a Baggie of drugs he claims he didn't ship.

"Very easy to explain, Your Honor," said Craig. "Those Baggies were from my house, where I used to live with [the roommate]. I don't know if he took something in the Baggies that I had touched in the home or whatever. Obviously, at some point in time, I touched the Baggies in that home before he sent them. That's the only explanation for it, because I didn't send anything anywhere."

After hearing Craig's testimony, the judge said she would think about the case over lunch.

"Should I decide to do this—and I'm not telling you whether I'm going to do it or not; I've only changed my mind sitting on the bench one other time—but should I decide to do this," the judge said, "you better talk with Mr. Thibodeaux, because you may truly wish that you were sitting in prison by the time I finish with you."

After the lunch break, the judge announced her decision.

Based on Craig's testimony, she was reducing his part in the drug transaction to a "minor role."

Craig Titus was not going to prison.

"Mr. Titus, it is not as good news as you think," the judge warned. "I told you if I did this, it was not going to be easy. In fact, Mr. Titus, you will see when I finish with this, you are going to end up spending more time visiting the United States Government than you would have had I left it the way it was. But it is this court's intention that you will not spend that time in prison."

Although she could have given him 10 to 16 months in prison, the judge sentenced Craig to 8 months in a halfway house and 8 months' home confinement, along with 3 years of supervised release. He was also forbidden to possess any illegal controlled substance and had to subject himself to regular testing to ensure that his body was free of drugs, including steroids.

He had to perform 300 hours of community service "within the athletic bodybuilding and health club environment, or hospice work, preferably with cancer patients" and immediately view videotape on the dangers of steroid use.

"I'm giving you an opportunity and the opportunity you asked me for," Judge Doherty said. "I'm giving you an opportunity to make a life. Mr. Titus, don't misunderstand: If I'm betting wrong on you and you test dirty, I'm putting you back in jail. Do you understand that?"

"Yes, ma'am," Craig said.

"Mr. Titus, I have given you the benefit of the doubt. I will not do that again."

At the end of the hearing, she sent him off with one more warning.

"Mr. Titus, pay attention to those films downstairs," she said. "Steroids in all likelihood will kill you. This court is adjourned."

WHEN *THE ADVOCATE* REPORTED ON THE SENTENCing, it referred to Craig as "a California man" and made no mention of his bodybuilding fame: the amateur victories, the Denver debacle, the magazine covers.

But word of Craig's sentencing swept through the bodybuilding community—not on the Internet; the chat rooms were still in their infancy then—but by telephone, at events and on the precursor to the Internet boards: the 1-900-PUMPIRON phone line.

"The feature that people used most often was the gossip feature," says bodybuilding journalist Ron Harris, who helped operate the line in the 1990s. "This was before the Internet, so this is how people got their news. They'd call up this stupid number for ninety-nine cents a minute, or a dollar ninety-nine, and hear all the dirt. I would write the scripts for it, we would gather the information through phone calls. So we put that on there, that thing about Craig."

Among those calling in to hear about the Craig Titus case was Craig Titus.

"I was in the office and took the call," Harris remembers. "He was deeply, deeply upset and he told me to take it off in a really mean, stern voice. He's got that deep, gravelly voice. He told me to take that off the phone number or else he would be at the office the next day with a baseball bat and 'use your imagination.'"

Harris, like everybody else, knew about Craig's Denver outburst and knew how angry he could get.

"I knew he wasn't a guy you wanted to mess around with," says Harris. "Not only that, he's two hundred and seventy pounds or whatever, so I told my boss, 'We need to take this stuff off.' So I'm pretty sure we did. It was off the next day and I didn't hear a thing about it again."

But as mad as Craig was at Harris, it was nothing compared to how he felt about John Romano, who, after his positive piece about Craig's troubles at the NPC show in Denver, wrote a tougher story about Craig's drug case.

"Without talking to me first, Romano wrote another

article stating that I was a rat. It was devastating to see this in an international magazine, or in any print, for that matter. He tore my character apart and I was not going to stand for it," Craig said. "Why in the hell was Romano so concerned if I was a rat or not?. . .

"Who in the hell does he think he is to judge me?"

Romano stood by his story, and eventually the storm passed, as it always did with Craig.

While this article appeared, Craig was serving out the first phase of his term in a halfway house in Inglewood, California, a middle-class community near Los Angeles International Airport, best known as the former home of the Los Angeles Lakers, who have since moved from the Forum to the Staples Center in downtown LA. According to news reports at the time, Craig had entered the halfway house on November 1, 1995, and would stay there for eight months.

As angry as Craig was, there was truth to the claim that he was ratting people out. During his October sentencing hearing, Craig acknowledged cooperating with authorities, traveling to Washington. His only frustration, it seemed, was that the feds didn't want more of his information—and that he had to keep paying his own travel bills.

This cooperation apparently continued while Craig was in the halfway house. According to court papers, while serving his sentence, Craig helped in a federal probe of a "large-scale systematic" theft of steroids from the Navy. Craig made undercover phone calls to people believed to have been involved in the thefts, the records said.

In any event, aside from his quarrels with Romano, Craig's sentence was not the hell that the judge had suggested. He quietly served his time, living up to the court's hopes of putting his life on the right course while treating his body well. He was able to continue training, keeping his weight and muscle mass at competitive levels, and by the time he was released, Craig Titus was in the best shape of his life.

The drug case, it turned out, would not end his career.

CHAPTER FOUR

BODYBUILDERS TALK ABOUT THE DAY THEY GET their pro card the same way others talk about their first kiss or their first baby.

Craig Titus had missed that precious moment by just one point that night in Denver. Now, one year—and one drug sentence—later, Craig had another shot.

On the weekend of June 28 and 29, 1996, a crowd of 2,000 screaming muscle-heads turned out at the Terrace Theater in Long Beach, California, for the NPC USA Men's Championships, featuring Craig Titus in his first competition since he had been sentenced on drug charges. People in the bodybuilding community, expecting to see him slimmed and weakened by the federal court system, were stunned to encounter a bulging Craig Titus at the competition.

No longer considered the favorite, especially since everybody assumed he was competing as a "natural bodybuilder," Craig had nothing to lose and everything to gain.

But this time Titus prevailed, edging out Tom Prince, himself an infamous figure in bodybuilding, who four years later would end up critically ill in the hospital when his kidneys gave out from years of painkillers and bodybuilding drugs.

On this day, however, Craig Titus had gone from the Bad Boy of Bodybuilding to the Comeback Kid.

"He looked great. It was the best I'd ever seen him," recalls Lonnie Teper. "He went into the halfway house—then won the USA! This is the most amazing thing. That's why I always called him the Teflon man. Nothing sticks. He bounces back from everything."

Emotion flowed out of Craig, only now it was gratitude and relief rather than rage.

"I turned pro and fulfilled my dream," Craig later said in an interview with MuscleNet. "I dedicated this victory to my son Aaron, who passed away in 1989."

Suddenly, everything was going Craig Titus' way. He had finished his stay in the halfway house and started 8 months of home confinement, which gave him greater leeway to work—and work out—as long as he got home in time and could account for his whereabouts.

It was, to be sure, a short leash. During this phase of his sentence, the US Attorney's Office filed a motion asking the judge to reduce his sentence. Prosecutors cited Craig's cooperation with the investigation into steroid theft by the Navy. But the judge denied the motion. She also turned down his request in October 1996 to travel to Dallas to sit in a booth signing autographs for a supplement called MET-Rx.

These were but small setbacks. Now possessing his pro card, Craig was able to enter the major contests: the Arnold and the Olympia.

He stood to easily make in the six figures, and the magazines still loved him, this convicted felon landing four major covers in 1996: *Muscle Mag International* in February, *Flex* and *Iron Man* in November and *Muscle Mag International* again in December.

The future was unlimited, all his dreams of fame and money within reach. The women adored him. The magazine writers clung to his every quote.

All he had to do was stay out of trouble.

CHAPTER FIVE

DR. SUI C. CHAN SAW A LOT OF URINE.

Gallons of it arrived every year at his Canadian lab, the Centre for Toxicology for the Calgary Regional Health Authority. The samples are identified only by numbers to preserve anonymity, meticulously tested for any number of illegal substances for the center's various customers, including the United States government, which contracted Chan's lab to test random urine samples of those in federal custody.

Over the years, Chan had found a lot of things in all that urine, but the sample that arrived on October 3, 1996, was something else.

The amount of the steroid testosterone contained in a urine sample is expressed as a ratio—the concentration of testosterone compared with a substance called epitestosterone. Nobody's really sure what epitestosterone does. It just sort of exists in the body, its sole use to science to serve as a benchmark for measuring testosterone.

The normal ratio in the male body of testosterone to epitestosterone is an even 1 to 1. Anything from 2 to 1 to 6 to 1 is considered unusually high, even suspicious as it reaches the higher range.

After 6, scientists consider the donor to have used testosterone.

In world-class cycling, a 4-to-1 ratio is out of bounds, as 2006 Tour de France winner Floyd Landis found when he was suspended by his team after his urine's ratio exceeded that limit.

In the urine sample that arrived at Dr. Chan's lab on October 3, the ratio was 50 to 1.

Whoever had peed in that vial was downing testosterone like Kool-Aid.

And the person had been doing so for months, going back to at least August.

In addition to testosterone, the urine sample contained what the lab considered a "high concentration" of boldenone, an oil-based injectible, legal only for veterinarians. This, again, had probably been used regularly since August.

Finally, there was a sign of stanozolol, also known as Winstrol, a tablet first used by vets to help weaken animals, but later made legal for humans by prescription. It was famously abused by Canadian Ben Johnson to run faster at the 1988 Olympics. He was later stripped of his gold medal in the 100 meters.

A few weeks after Dr. Chan got that heavily juiced sample in October, the probation department informed Craig Titus that one of his randomly collected urine samples had tested dirty. According to the lab analysis, Craig likely had juiced up just weeks after—though quite possibly before—winning the USAs and getting his pro card—while he was still in home confinement and under strict orders by the judge to stay off the steroids or face a one-way ticket to federal prison.

Strangely, even after Craig was notified of the positive tests, he continued to provide urine samples in the fall of 1996—and continued to test dirty. His testosterone level in mid-November, after notification, was actually higher than the month before; in fact, it was the second-highest level Dr. Chan's lab had seen all year out of 700 samples.

In that same November sample, the lab found the fourth-highest level in the complex's history of nandrolone metabolites, a sign of steroid use. And Craig's level of boldenone was the year's highest for the lab. He also tested positive for methandienone, a prescription tablet steroid used for building up muscle.

Craig provided more samples in December 1996 and January 1997, and more positive tests came back.

According to the lab, these levels clearly signaled that Craig was juicing up, even as he was providing samples that he knew were being tested. One test also showed that his epitestosterone had also skyrocketed, normally a sign that the subject is taking supplements of that to try to mask the testosterone.

If the analysis was correct, it would be a case of breathtaking brashness—and self-destruction.

Meanwhile, Craig's temper had returned. Throughout 1997, he was as belligerent as anybody had ever seen him. In January, he punched an NPC light-heavyweight in Gold's Gym in Venice Beach for saying "the wrong things," according to Craig.

"I knocked the shit out of him," he boasted to *Flex* magazine.

It was one of several scuffles that people could recall.

"I saw him on July 4, 1997," recalls Lonnie Teper. "He was walking around without his shirt, with this babe on his arm. He just really hated Shawn Ray at the time. I don't remember why. But he would talk about it. When people asked when he was going to compete, again, he would say, 'I want to stand next to Shawn Ray. I want to kick Shawn Ray's ass.'"

Craig would have to wait for his chance.

"That month," Teper said, "is when he got popped."

JUST THREE WEEKS AFTER RUNNING INTO TEPER, Craig was back in Lafayette, Louisiana.

When Craig Titus had last stood before US District Judge Rebecca Doherty nearly two years earlier, Doherty had been tough, but fair. She'd gone the extra mile to find a way to keep him out of prison, giving him the benefit of the doubt, both on the amount of drugs and Craig's culpability. She had ended that hearing in October 1995 with a stern warning that if he tested dirty, "I'm putting you back in jail."

Now, on Friday, July 25, 1997, Craig was back before Doherty in a test of both her patience and her memory. The United States Probation Office filed a petition seeking the revocation of his supervised release, alleging six violations of the condition to remain drug-free, occurring between October 1996 and January 1997. Craig's probation officer, Mark Coleman, formally informed him of the dirty tests on April 3.

Anonymous no more, the local paper pointed out in its report that Craig Titus was the reigning 1996 National

Physique Committee USA Champion of both the men's heavyweight and overall titles.

Doherty called the hearing to order, to determine whether to send Craig to prison on a probation violation. The first witness for the prosecution was Dr. Sui Chan.

Chan gave his lengthy title—director of the Centre of Toxicology for the Calgary Regional Health Authority, under contract by the US Probation Office to test for anabolic steroids—and his impressive credentials— steroids consultant for the National Football League in the United States and head of the steroid testing program for the 1998 Winter Olympic games in his hometown of Calgary, Alberta.

He then nailed Craig.

Under questioning by Assistant US Attorney Luke Walker, who just the year before had asked the judge to cut short Craig's sentence for his cooperation, Chan recited the test results showing the high concentrations of various steroids in Craig's samples from the fall of 1996 and early 1997, including the elevated epitestosterone, signifying an effort to mask steroid use.

During cross-examination, defense attorney Gregory Thibodeaux sought to show that Craig's case was unique.

"Dr. Chan," he asked, "how many bodybuilders have you tested at your laboratory?"

"I really don't know the people I'm testing, because there's no name," the doctor replied. "Only identified by numbers. So I don't know whether they are bodybuilders or athletes. So I have no idea."

"Is it possible that the steroids could have been stored in his system and then excreted on those dates?"

Chan said no, "Not to this level."

Craig's defense was that his body had stored steroids taken much earlier, before the judge told him not to at the sentencing, and then the steroids were unexpectedly released into his body.

This happened, the defense claimed, because of Craig's peculiar bodybuilder physiology. The defense said the steroids got socked away in scar tissue from the old steroid injection sites, then broke free during one of Craig's massage sessions. At the same time, Craig was losing body weight, making the old steroid concentrations, from when he was heavier, look worse than they really were.

"Is it possible," Thibodeaux asked Dr. Chan, "because some steroids are stored in fat, is it possible that if a person were to have rapid weight loss, that these steroids would then be released into his system?"

"Theoretically possible," acknowledged Chan. "But I don't have any knowledge, direct knowledge of that. And among our circle, no one has given the opinion that we can obtain such a level by losing body weight."

During redirect testimony, Chan told prosecutor Walker that he didn't think there would be any difference between the specimens of bodybuilders and other people, and that "no one has the opinion that they are different, except that they tend to use more" steroids.

Chan did nothing to help. Craig would have to try to talk himself out of this predicament.

The defense called Craig Titus to the stand.

"Mr. Titus," his lawyer asked, "how are you employed?"

"Professional bodybuilder with the International Federation of Bodybuilding."

"Have you used anabolic steroids in the past?" asked Thibodeaux.

"Absolutely," said Craig.

Providing even more information about his steroid practices as he did in the 1995 hearing, Craig explained that he'd started using steroids from the very beginning of his career, beginning in 1988, when he'd won his first competition, the Houston Bodybuilding Championship, then "off-and-on" until 1991, when he was starting to make his mark in regional contests. The use became daily, he said, in the four years leading up to the USAs in Denver.

"How would you take these steroids?" his lawyer asked.

"By injection," Craig said. "It's safer than tablet because it's not digested."

"What is involved when you inject a steroid into your body?"

"You take a . . . three-cc syringe, one-and-a-half inch, draw the oil base steroid out of the multi-use vial and inject it to various sites in the body: shoulders, quadriceps, gluteus, calves," Craig said. "Once in the morning and once at night, because it's time-released."

"How much would you administer with one syringe?"

"It would be two syringes a day, about six to eight cc's of steroids a day."

Craig insisted, however that he'd stopped the frequent steroid injections when he was ordered to by the judge back in 1995. He was well aware that he couldn't take them anymore, after "I had to watch a one-hour tape on steroids" following his sentencing.

Even at the time, Craig said, he was concerned that the steroids would remain in his system when the random testing began, and right after his sentencing he asked his probation officer to test him for steroids to provide a bascline for future tests.

"They could see the various drugs in my system so that they would know what's in my system and what would be going away in my system," said Titus. "They would decrease over a long period of time."

But he wasn't tested then. Craig said he did know that later, while on supervised release, he was being tested. He said that on October 3, 1996, during a random test, he'd seen the lady at the testing facility check the box marked "steroids" on his form.

The testing had come, he said, during a time of profound change in his body. He said that from July 1996 to January 1997, his weight had dropped from 271 pounds to 226. Around the same time, he'd begun massage therapy.

"I had cysts all over my body," said Craig. "From what the massage therapist told me, they were scar tissue. Cocoon-like scar tissue is what they call it."

The judge asked, "Cocoon-like?"

"Cocoon-like, or systemic, I believe the word is," answered Craig. "That's what the massage therapists were telling me it was, because I was concerned with the knots I had all over my body."

Craig's attorney asked, "Did you know that you had these prior to this weight loss?"

"Well, I knew I had injection sites that were sore," Craig said, "but I didn't realize I had cysts and scar tissue building up over the years of use until I lost the weight."

"And what are these scar tissue sites?" his lawyer asked.

"All I can tell you is what I was told by the doctors."

"What did they tell you?"

"They told me there was scar tissue buildup from the needles going in from the massive use over and over again, and then the drugs, along with the scar tissue, all combined in one big knot in my muscle," said Craig. "In other words, I was sticking a needle back into scar tissue that was already there and filling it with whatever I was shooting into it."

"In fact, you were injecting steroids into the scar tissue?"

"Yes, and I was thinking it was muscle."

"Are these lesions painful?"

"They don't hurt until they are getting rubbed on by deep tissue therapy," said Craig. "They actually break them. You can actually hear the sound of them breaking them open."

"Is there any other way to remove the scar tissue sites?" Thibodeaux asked.

"Surgery, they actually make an incision and remove the scar tissue. But the doctors told me to try the massage therapy first, which has been effective."

"What happens in the massage therapy?"

"I go in two or three times a week, mostly just twice a week because it's very painful," Craig said. "And they massage you, take the scar tissue between their hands, their knuckles, their hands, and they break the scar tissue down. And then by continuing massage therapy, it goes away. And it's assimilated into the body."

"Did your massage therapist tell you that it's possible that the toxins that are in that scar tissue are going to be released into your body?"

Prosecutor Luke Walker had heard enough.

"Objection," the prosecutor said. "A massage therapist is now giving an expert opinion that he has not demonstrated the massage therapist has."

"Sustained," Judge Doherty said.

Changing course, Craig's attorney returned to asking him about his history of steroid use. The first time he'd gotten them legally was from a physician in 1995.

"And what were they prescribed for?" asked his attorney.

"Impotency," Craig said. "I was experiencing impotency from the use of steroids."

"And what steroid was prescribed?"

"Methyltestosterone," Craig answered, referring to a synthetic androgenic steroid.

Craig said he hadn't just used that steroid for his love life, but started using it in mid-September 1995 to help heal a torn shoulder muscle.

The judge reacted sharply: "Did we not chat about the steroid usage at your guilty plea, Mr. Titus?" she asked, referring to a hearing in April 1995.

"Yes, we did," acknowledged Craig.

"And yet you used steroids between the guilty plea and the sentencing? Am I correct?"

"I used the remainder of the methyltestosterone for my chest that I tore."

"And those steroids had not been prescribed to you for that purpose by any physician? Am I correct?" the judge asked.

"Yes, you are correct," Craig said. "I used the methyltestosterone that was prescribed for my impotency."

Craig insisted that he didn't take any steroids—for his chest or impotency or anything else in late 1996 during his supervised release.

"I sure didn't go and take more testosterone before November knowing that I was testing in October," he said. "I didn't know I tested positive, but I knew I was being tested."

Trying to exonerate Craig, Thibodeaux asked, "You've been truthful with the court regarding your use of steroids in the past, have you not?"

"Yes," said Craig.

His lawyer asked Craig if he had ever taken the masking steroid epitestosterone.

"No," said Craig. "I read about it on the Internet. I've never even seen it."

Incredulous, the judge jumped in.

"You mean you were not, as a bodybuilder, aware that the manner in which one is tested for testosterone and the determination of a positive finding is made by way of ratio between testosterone and epitestosterone?" she asked.

"Absolutely, I'm aware of the fact of the ratios, how they are tested," said Craig. "But as a bodybuilder, there is no way I could mask my testosterone with the epitestosterone, because my testosterone levels, when I was taking, are way greater than anybody, than the testing facilities, test."

Craig said he was so loaded with testosterone, there "is no possible way" he could mask it.

"I've taken all these steroids up here except the epitestosterone," he said. "I'm not denying that I've taken these steroids. . . . I'm not denying that I've taken these steroids."

He said that what he *was* denying was that he'd taken steroids in late 1996 in violation of his supervised release.

During cross-examination, prosecutor Walker asked Craig to elaborate on his steroid history, asking him which steroids he had taken over the course of his career.

Craig rattled off a medicine chest full.

"Liquid Anadrol. Oxymetholone, which is a tablet, Anavar. I've used a tablet form of andriol, which is a tablet form of testosterone. Clenbuterol, which isn't necessarily a steroid, but is classified in the same way. It's used for body fat. That's basically about it."

Walker didn't bother with definitions.

"And you were using these in 1989, 1990, 1991, all through that time period?" the prosecutor asked.

"Yeah. The ones I just named especially because those were the ones available earlier in my career."

"And you used these steroids on up until, basically, you got caught?"

"These, when I got caught, yeah," Craig said.

"Your career is as a bodybuilder?" the prosecutor asked.

"Yes, sir."

"And in your career as a bodybuilder, you are going to have to take steroids to be competitive?"

"Yes, sir."

"So if you are going to continue to be a bodybuilder, you have to continue to take steroids? Otherwise, you will lose the weight and you will not be able to be competitive?"

"Yes, sir," Craig said, "but not while under supervised release."

"So your intention is to not use steroids until you finish supervised release, and then you will continue to use steroids after that point? That way you can continue to be competitive?"

"This is what I *intend* to do," Craig said, correcting him. "I intend to compete next year and see how I do as a natural bodybuilder without the use of drugs. If I can continue to compete on a competitive level and stay in there, then it's not going to be necessary for me to take them."

"But your intention at this point is, if you can't compete as a natural bodybuilder, you are then going to . . . continue to use steroids?"

"I'm not going to lie," Craig said. "Absolutely. I've thought about that."

He had sufficient incentive, saying that he expected to make more than $100,000 that year, his first year as a pro.

"You would agree with me," Walker asked, "that if your supervised release was revoked by Judge Doherty, that would be very detrimental to your career?"

"It would be the worst thing for me."

Walker asked if he knew about bodybuilders who "get away" with using steroids.

Craig suggested that the prosecutor was missing the

point: There was nothing to get away with in professional bodybuilding.

"If they haven't been in trouble," said Craig, "and they are not being tested, they are going to use enhancing drugs."

"Don't you also know about athletes that can beat the test?" asked Walker.

"Yes, I do."

"It's possible to beat the test?"

"Not as a bodybuilder."

"Why not?"

"Because the dosages aren't even close. They are much, much greater as a bodybuilder," said Craig. "A bodybuilder wouldn't use epitestosterone to mask. A track athlete, Olympic wrestler, Olympic power-lifting athlete would use epitestosterone to mask the testosterone because it's a minimal amount, very minuscule."

When Craig's attorney returned to ask additional questions, Craig insisted that he was now trying to make it as a pro steroid-free.

"The natural bodybuilders don't do as well in the competition," said Craig, "but they still make good money on other things like appearances, magazine articles, and photo shoots."

To bolster his steroids-released-from-cysts theory, Craig called as a witness Dr. James E. Wright, a consultant in the health and fitness industry and president of the Sports Science Consultants, which Wright said "do concept and product, research development and marketing in the health and fitness industry."

Although offered as an expert witness, Wright said he was not a medical doctor, but held a PhD in zoology with "a specialty in physiology." The doctorate came from Mississippi State University. He said his specialty for the last twenty years was the use of ergogenic or performance-enhancing drugs. He'd written a book in 1977 while doing post-doctorate work at UC Santa Barbara called *Anabolic Steroids in Sports*.

"Have you ever been recognized by a court of law as an expert in sports physiology?" asked defense attorney Thibodeaux.

"I've served as an expert witness as part of my business," Wright said.

"That's not the question," Judge Doherty interjected. "He's asked you whether or not you have presented in court—had your qualifications presented and you have been accepted within court, not in a deposition, as an expert. In court as an expert in sports physiology?"

"No," Wright conceded.

With this foundation, the defense asked that he be accepted as "an expert in the field of sports physiology with a specialty of performance-enhancing use of drugs."

The prosecution didn't object—Walker could do his damage during cross-examination—but the judge had some concerns.

"I'm not sure," she said. "I need to understand exactly what you do, Doctor."

Wright went over his qualifications again, this time adding that for five years he had been the Chief of Strength Research at the US Army Institute of Environmental Medicine, "working on ways to maintain and enhance performance in military personnel."

"You are not a toxicologist, pharmacologist, not a medical doctor or a chemist?" the judge asked.

"No, no, no, no," he said. "Practical experience in studies as a member of the US military, plus twenty-five years of reading in this area as well as contact with other professionals in this field have given me a much broader base and knowledge than would be expected from a narrow discipline of laboratory science."

"Or zoology," the judge said.

"Right."

Wright also conceded he had done no original research on steroids in the body, but he had read the articles.

"I have about twenty in my briefcase," he said.

Reluctantly, the judge accepted him as an expert.

Testifying on direct examination, Wright said that Craig Titus had contacted him in March 1997 when Craig was told his urine had tested positive for steroids. After a meeting, Wright examined Craig and offered "different possibilities or explanations for the appearance of these drugs."

One of those possible explanations was the one Craig was offering at this hearing.

"Having examined Mr. Titus and palpated the areas of adhesion and scar tissue all over his body," Wright said, "it is completely plausible to me that within these pockets of scar tissue boluses of injected drugs have been sequestered for long periods of time and released with this continued pattern of deep tissue massage."

"Doctor," the judge asked, "is there any study out there or any published material that says that what you are saying is plausible, has in fact occurred or does in fact occur?"

"There are no published studies," Wright said. "But there has been no research."

Wright insisted that bodybuilders "are a class unto themselves" and that there are "even subclasses within bodybuilders that are very cliquey and closed-mouth about their drug-use habits, and who would never participate in such studies."

But he said that, anecdotally, bodybuilders have much more steroid-trapping lesions than other people from all the shots they get. He said it would not be uncommon for a bodybuilder to inject himself three, four or more times a day with steroids and insulin. He said that other athletes don't take as many steroids, and can mask them with epitestosterone, because they still need to perform.

"It's only bodybuilders that are not performance-oriented, but want to blow up muscle mass to sort of a super-physiologic effect from these super-physiologic doses," he said.

The effect, Wright said, could also be psychological.

"Most people that get to a very high level are not satisfied," he said. "They still want to get bigger. So cutting back is like taking the baby away from the bottle. I'm not sure that's an appropriate analogy, but it can be very, very traumatic. Even though they can maintain [size], no one wants to maintain. Everybody that's in the gym, training hours and hours a day, sleeping, eating bizarre diets—from a normal person's perspective—and making that level of a commitment, is not going to want to maintain. They want to be all they can be. They've sold their soul as well as their body, so to speak."

But what about the masking agent, epitestosterone? the judge asked. How could that be present in Craig's body when he claimed he'd never used it?

"I believe he never used it," Wright said. "I don't know anyone in bodybuilding that ever has. They don't need to."

"That is not answering my question," the judge said.

"Well, we really don't know what the source [is]," said Wright. "It seems to be an innocuous substance. It's just there. It probably has some function, but we don't know what it is."

Under cross-examination, Wright acknowledged he had been paid to give a favorable opinion.

"He hired you?" asked Walker.

"That's correct."

"He came to you and said, 'I flunked a drug test, but I haven't used drugs since June or all of 'ninety-five, can you help me explain how I got these positive tests?' "

"Correct."

"And you took his word for it that he had not used steroids during that time period?"

"That's correct."

"And your opinion is not based on any type of scientific testing, right?"

"That's correct."

"It's just some theory that some people have formulated, correct?"

"That's correct."

IT DIDN'T TAKE LONG FOR THE JUDGE TO RULE.

"The government has proved by a preponderance of the evidence that the defendant possessed a controlled substance, and as such, he violated the condition of his supervised release," Judge Doherty said.

Calling Wright "Mister," not "Doctor," she characterized his explanation as an "unsupported and unsubstantiated theory" that could not even account for the presence of epitestosterone. She noted that Wright had no peer review articles, no evidence within the medical or scientific community to support his theory and could at best only rely upon anecdote.

The judge then stared down at Craig.

"Mr. Titus," she said, "I think I was perfectly clear with you each time you came before me that the rules did apply to you. I think I also was perfectly clear, Mr. Titus, that if you broke those rules, I would do what was necessary so that you would understand that the rules do apply to you."

Becoming increasingly agitated, Craig started speaking.

"Mr. Titus," the judge shot back, "I am not inviting you to interrupt me at this time. Mr. Titus, you have convinced this court that you think you can beat the system. You cannot. Your supervised release is revoked. You are sentenced to two years in prison."

Craig's lawyer asked if he could be allowed to "take care of matters in California," but the judge wouldn't let him.

"You are remanded to the custody of the United States Marshal to begin service, Mr. Titus," said the judge.

As he was being led away in handcuffs, Craig's emotions overwhelmed him. He bit his finger until it bled.

"Oh, my God," he said. "I did not do this."

◆ ◆ ◆

THAT NIGHT, CRAIG ENDED UP IN THE HOSPITAL ward, not for the hurt finger, but after telling a nurse that he had to detox from painkillers. This was just hours after he'd told the judge under oath that he had been clean for months.

By Monday, July 28, 1997, Craig was back before Judge Doherty with a lot of explaining to do.

The judge asked him why he'd gone to the hospital. Craig, seated at the counsel table, started to speak, but the judge said, "Mr. Titus, please stand if you are going to address me."

Getting to his feet, Craig said, "Your Honor, on the way to the jail, I was told by one of the guards if I said I was detoxing for pain relievers, they would keep me on the medical floor and put me on the first floor instead of putting me in the population, so my life wouldn't be living hell."

Craig said he "took the advice of one of the guards" and pretended to need the detox.

"You lied," the judge shot back, "and you said that you were in fact addicted to painkillers, when you are telling me now that is not the case?"

"No," Craig admitted, "I didn't take painkillers, no."

"But you chose to lie so that you could get better treatment? Am I correct?" the judge asked.

"I chose to lie because I had never been in prison," Craig said. "I didn't want to go into population. It's not someplace I find very delightful."

"It's not designed to be delightful, Mr. Titus."

"I understand that."

"Let me make certain I understand this," said the

judge, now livid. "The marshals then went through all of the trouble and time to pack you up and take you to the hospital and sit and wait with you for two hours while you were engaged in attempting to receive medical treatment for something that you were not in fact in crisis upon? Is that correct?"

"No," said Craig. "I was sick, Your Honor. I was throwing up and had diarrhea from being upset from going to jail."

"But you in fact did refuse treatment after you got there, did you not?"

"They kept me there two-and-a-half hours and wouldn't look at me, and one of the marshals suggested I go back to the jail and lay down in the bunk where it's much warmer and easier to throw up in the toilet than sitting in the cold cage in the hospital."

"Which particular marshal was it that told you you need not stay? Can you describe him or her for me?"

"I don't remember."

"Was it a marshal?"

"It was a guard."

"So it was not one of my marshals. It was one of the personnel from the correctional institute, Lafayette Parish correctional institute?"

"Yes, ma'am."

"So if I were to look on the log, I could determine who it was that went with you to the hospital facility?"

"Your Honor, I don't recall who told me that."

"But it was someone from that facility that went with you, am I correct?"

"They didn't go with me, no, Your Honor."

"This person just happened to be at the hospital?"

Craig tried to explain further, but got nowhere with the judge. She spoke to one of her marshals, who said Craig had been transported from the jail, but he didn't know who had escorted him. He said he could check the records, but needed a court order because it was a medical matter.

"I want them," Judge Doherty said. "It is so ordered."

"Yes, ma'am," the marshal said.

Turning back to Craig, the judge said, "I strongly suggest that you stop lying."

"I didn't lie when I was in here Friday," Craig said.

"I strongly suggest you stop lying," she repeated. "It is a very serious thing to admit to being addicted to painkillers."

She said she would speak to whomever Craig saw and will review the records and "I'm going to be very interested" in comparing Craig's version with what she finds.

"I strongly suggest you stop attempting to manipulate the system," she said. "That has been your pattern and that has been your problem since I have been engaged with you. So I strongly suggest you stop."

Then, after castigating Craig, the judge gave him one small break. Doherty said she stood by her decision to put Craig in prison, and she believed the government had proven its case that he had taken steroids while on supervised release, but she gave him the option of going to a doctor, a real medical doctor—not a zoologist—for an examination, to see once and for all whether weight loss or massage therapy could be the cause of the dirty steroid tests.

"The only reason, quite frankly, that I am doing this at this point is because I have concern as to whether or not Mr. Titus has not convinced himself that this [steroid use] is the case," the judge said. "And if he doesn't straighten it out in his own mind, I don't see him benefiting from this in any fashion. Because if he doesn't learn the rules apply to him, he's going to be back again before some other judge, and it's going to be for a much more extended stay."

Two weeks later, Craig was back, again, before this judge, who by now had obtained the records of Craig's jail transfer and hospital stay, and had spoken to her marshal. Yet another story now emerged of what had happened between court and the jail after Craig's hearing. It turned out that at the hospital, Craig had threatened to hurt himself if he had to go into the regular prison population, and was put on suicide watch. The nurse made this notation on his chart: "Will harm self if I have jail time."

There was no evidence that a guard had told Craig to fake a drug dependency to get out of the prison, or that Craig himself had ever claimed that. In fact, Craig had only complained about cold sweats and nausea from taking Vicodin tablets for a degenerative disc in his lower back. Then, when the nurse tried to admit Craig to the hospital, he'd changed his mind and said he wanted to go back to prison.

"Inmate stated he did not want to sit there being uncomfortable and cold," the nurse's notes said.

Craig even had to sign a waiver saying he was ignoring medical advice and requesting a trip back to a cell. He was given 15 cc's of nausea relief medication and sent along his way.

The judge completed her account of the investigation into Craig's activities without comment, letting the facts speak for themselves. She then moved on to Craig's visit to a local physician, Dr. Christopher Lee. After examining Craig, the doctor wrote the judge that he found "not much validity" to the claim the steroids were released from scar tissue during massages unless somebody could find a study to back that up. According to Judge Doherty, the doctor said that scar tissue is full of blood vessels that would have flushed away the steroids as in any other bodily tissue.

"Therefore," Judge Doherty concluded, "this court finds that that which was presented by Dr. Lee in no way changes this court's prior ruling: that the government has proved with a preponderance of the evidence that Mr. Titus engaged in taking steroids during the time when he was on supervised release in direct violation of this court's order."

The judge minced no words.

"It seems Mr. Titus tends to believe his own press," said the judge, "and to rule out any possible chance that there might be some validity to this hypothesis that his own expert could give no underlying background for any study or any medical testimony, any medical journal, medical scholarly article—nothing other than a hypothesis from a zoology major."

This ordinarily would have ended the hearing, but Craig was not done irritating the judge. He now announced that he was dumping his lawyer, Gregory Thibodeaux, in favor of the similar-sounding Jason Robideaux.

The judge asked the new lawyer wearily, "You were asked by Mr. Titus to be engaged as his counsel, am I correct?"

"Yes, Your Honor," said Robideaux.

"Did he intend to pay you?"

"I assume so, Your Honor—or friends of his."

"Mr. Titus, please stand," Judge Doherty said. "How is it that your financial condition has changed so radically that throughout the entirety of these proceedings you were unable to pay an attorney, but now you are able to pay an attorney? What has changed?"

Craig explained that back in October 1995, he didn't have the money, so he used Thibodeaux at taxpayers' expense. He was now taking out a loan from friends, he said.

The judge didn't believe him. She said that "based upon your lack of credibility," she was referring the matter to a magistrate judge to evaluate Craig's finances and make a recommendation on whether Craig should reimburse the Federal Public Defender's Office.

Doherty then turned to the lawyer, and said, "Mr. Robideaux, as far as this court is concerned, this matter is complete. So I don't really know for what purpose or at what state you feel that you are enrolling."

Robideaux said he had "several things" for the court to consider. If she doesn't, then he would sign on as an appellate lawyer.

"I hope this court is aware I've never presented Your Honor anything that I would consider the court would consider frivolous," he said. "But I think there are some issues that need to be presented to the court that should have been presented."

"Let me interrupt," the judge said. "I think Mr. Thibodeaux did a very good job for Mr. Titus. In fact, if Mr. Thibodeaux hadn't been with Mr. Titus early on,

Mr. Titus probably would not have ended up in a halfway house. And Mr. Thibodeaux came at times when he knew he was likely to raise the ire of the court. . . . And you know, like the good soldier and the good attorney and the good advocate ought to do, he sat there and took it."

Robideaux said he understood all that and also understood that now he, too, was about to feel the court's ire. But, like his predecessor, he marched on, saying that he had some new information about steroid testing. The judge said to put it in writing—once he actually becomes Craig's lawyer of record after the financial matters are settled.

"Let me tell you, Mr. Robideaux," the judge warned, "you haven't been down this path with us. It's been a very, very long path."

She urged him to read the transcripts and note that she had warned Craig not to take steroids, but he had anyway. She'd given him the benefit of the doubt at various junctures, and he still did wrong.

"He has been less than forthright with this court. He, in all likelihood, has committed perjury before this court. He has lied with impunity," she said. "It has been a very long path, Mr. Robideaux, one which at every turn I have given Mr. Titus the benefit of the doubt. Those days now are complete. He has convinced me that he believes the rules do not apply to him, that he is above them, that he need not comply with them and that he can manipulate this system to his benefit and his desire. He is in error.

"Mr. Titus," she said, "I meant what I said about Mr. Thibodeaux," she said. "He's what got you to that halfway house to begin with. Don't think he blew it. He did not. You blew it."

With that, Craig went off to prison—for the next year.

There would be no furloughs for competitions, no breaks of any sort. There would be no major magazine covers in 1997 and 1998.

He did his time at Lompoc penitentiary, in central California, and the bodybuilding industry went on without him.

For all the attention he garnered, all the controversy he generated, the fact remained that Craig had won only one important title, and his future, as he neared his 33rd birthday, looked grim. The magazines latched on to other stars, other story lines.

"Craig wasn't really a big impact on the industry," recalls Shawn Ray. "He didn't have a following, so to speak. He was a new kid on the block and he was a guy that I knew was coming and the judges knew was coming, but I don't think the fans really cared much, because it didn't affect them. A year later we got another USA Champion, so as quickly as he came, he disappeared."

Shawn Ray underestimated Craig Titus.

Craig would launch a comeback, only this time he wouldn't do it alone.

CHAPTER SIX

THE FIRST TIME HE SAW HER, HE WOULD LATER TELL interviewers, was on the afternoon of November 16, 1995. At the time, Craig Titus was a convicted felon, about to begin an 8-month sentence in a halfway house and another 8 months in home confinement, on the drug charge.

On this fall day in Southern California, Craig took a break from his troubles to attend a women's fitness competition in Redondo Beach, just down the 405 freeway from the Inglewood halfway house.

He joined other bodybuilding friends watching the Fitness America Pageant national championships, a female variation of the men's bodybuilding competition, in which the women are judged on their physiques, flexibility and athleticism. The highlight of every fitness event is the short routine in which the women don theatrical costumes or sparkly leotards for a high-energy gymnastics/cheerleading act set to music.

"Kelly Ryan came out on stage with a routine that I will never forget," Craig later told Ron Avidan at Getbig.com. "It was to 'Popeye the Sailor Man.' I was with

Shawn Ray and a few other pros, and we thought that she was the cutest damn thing that we had ever seen."

Craig couldn't stop talking about this Kelly Ryan, and told his friends he wanted to meet her after the show.

He wasn't the only one impressed.

At age 23, Kelly Ryan was the rising star of women's fitness. Although considered average on physique—her short, boxy gymnast's body lacked the V-taper the judges so adored, even for women—Kelly was drawing attention for her acrobatic, skillfully choreographed routines that had the crowd roaring. She also had a megawatt smile, engaging personality and a leaping ability that would soon earn her the nickname Flyin' Ryan.

Craig's friends said he didn't stand a chance with her. She was the darling of fitness and he was already known as Bodybuilding's Bad Boy. Not even Craig's powers as a player would work on somebody as sweet as Kelly Ryan.

Undaunted, Craig tracked Kelly down after the competition—she finished tied for sixth on the judging, but got among the loudest ovations—and tried to talk to her backstage.

"But she was with her parents . . . and she didn't leave her mom and dad's side," Craig recalled, "so I couldn't talk to her."

After that day, their lives took different courses—Craig's through the federal penal system, Kelly's to heights she'd never dreamed of.

ALTHOUGH SHE HAD THE REPUTATION AS THE southern belle of fitness, Kelly Ryan actually grew up a little bit of everywhere. She was born on July 10, 1972, in Minneapolis, Minnesota, but wouldn't stay there long. Her father, Thomas, worked in marketing for the Ford Motor Company, and was frequently transferred, taking with him the Ryan clan—Kelly's mother, Norma, who went by Niki, then a homemaker, and older brother Mike. There were stops in Michigan, Seattle, Jacksonville, Florida, and Houston, where Kelly finished elementary school and attended middle school.

Athletically gifted from the start, Kelly began gymnastics at age 5, and when the family moved to Texas, she trained under famed coach Bela Karolyi, who had guided Nadia Comaneci to the Olympics.

Among those training with Kelly was an older girl named Mary Lou Retton, who would go on to Olympic glory and cereal box cover fame.

Although Karolyi would give Kelly a gymnastics foundation that would serve her well during a successful professional career, her memories of toiling under the Romanian's tutelage weren't always pleasant.

"When I was nine, he was training me for the Olympics for the years ahead," Kelly said in a February 2000 interview with AlluringFitness.com. "I was about two age groups behind Mary Lou Retton. He always started us really, really young and that's pretty much when all the high pressure was on. . . . We'd train before elementary school, after elementary school, on weekends."

As a middle-schooler, Kelly was not only involved in gymnastics, but joined the swim team and played soccer, volleyball and basketball. When she finished middle school, her family was to make another move—this time to South Carolina—and Kelly had to decide at age 13 whether to stay in Houston with another family to attend high school and continue her gymnastics training. She opted to leave Karolyi behind.

"At the time I was just really burned out and was having problems, little bit with ulcers and stuff from the stress," she told AlluringFitness.com.

In the new high school, she continued to play volleyball, basketball and soccer—her mother was her soccer coach—and joined the cheerleading squad At her mother's urging, Kelly developed interests not only in nutrition, but in bodybuilding, which was unusual for girls at her school.

Kelly once recalled how her mother went into the principal's office to tell him that Kelly would be better served by taking a bodybuilding class than physics. "My school was very academically oriented. It was so old-fashioned Southern values," she told AlluringFitness.com "He was like: 'She is going to be one of the only girls in [bodybuilding].' My mom's like: 'I don't care.'"

Her mother, Kelly said, felt weight training would strengthen her daughter mentally as much as physically.

It was a cheerleading scholarship that brought her to the University of South Carolina, in Columbia. She joined the Zeta Tau Alpha sorority and studied journalism, mass communications and her father's business, marketing. She captained USC's varsity cheer squad for two years and headed the school's dance team, which called themselves the Southern Belles.

While on the outside a model student and picture of health, Kelly had not resolved the emotional problems plaguing her in Houston, and by her late teens her body and mind were at war in the form of bulimia, the disorder marked by binge eating, followed by binge vomiting.

She hit the worst stretch during college when she finally sought help in a hospital rehab program. Years later, she spoke about bulimia in the same way she talked about everything else: straightforwardly, no-nonsense, approaching it like her fitness career—a challenge that must be addressed positively.

When a bulimia sufferer wrote in to Kelly's online advice column, "Kelly Ryan's Corner," she said, "You can overcome Bulimia with knowledge and trust in yourself." Calling bulimia a "tricky disorder" linked to "control issues," Kelly said, "I used to deprive myself of a lot of types of food. This deprivation turns into the loss of control and creates binge eating."

With help, Kelly overcame bulimia, neared graduation and started thinking about her future. She considered moving to California to pursue a career in marketing and advertising like her father, while also trying out for the Laker Girls, the cheerleaders for the NBA team. "That didn't work out," she told AlluringFitness.com, and set her sights on something else closer to home.

Yet, the answer lay closer to cheerleading than she might have imagined. In 1995—around the time that Craig Titus was pleading guilty to drug charges—Kelly Ryan saw her first women's fitness show on ESPN. It changed her life. Within months, she would have a chance to compete.

Ken Taylor, the strength coach for Kelly's university cheerleading squad—as well as a trainer at the local

World Gym and promoter of local bodybuilding exhibitions—added an element to his annual South Carolina state bodybuilding show: a women's fitness competition.

The female talent pool was so small that Taylor asked the cheerleaders and dance squad members to compete. A member of both squads, Kelly Ryan plunged in with characteristic enthusiasm, slipping on a neon-yellow bikini and dyed neon-yellow shoes—"What was I thinking?" she later joked—for an energetic fitness routine, full of leaps and flips and tumbling, to the *William Tell* Overture.

In her debut, she placed first out of thirteen competitors, and her future seemed determined.

She started working as an instructor at a local studio called The Firm, learning more sophisticated weight-training regimens, and showed up in the evenings at World Gym. It was there that she met Keith Kephart, a former big-time college football strength coach now working as one of the most sought-after personal trainers in the South.

"One of the other trainers just sort of introduced us, and Kelly is one of those people that you immediately like," recalls Kephart. "She had it all. She had the work ethic. She had the mentality. She was driven. And she pushed when people would normally shut down, quit, too much, can't do it. Not her. She had great tenacity. She loved the challenge. She would not back off. And yet she had the genetic capability, muscular-wise and physique-wise, for that to take place. She's probably one of the best athletes I've ever trained."

Taking on Kelly as a client, Kephart reviewed

videos of her routines and was impressed with her athletic skills: her leaping and flexibility, stage presence and overall charisma were world-class. But he knew that for women's fitness competition she needed more. Although in its infancy—the NPC had not yet sponsored a women's event—the sport already had specific demands: it favored women who were buff, flexible and, most important, able to pull off a short physical fitness routine that combined skills used in cheerleading, dance and gymnastics.

Kelly's background in all three placed her at a distinct advantage, as did her exuberant personality, which would play well to the crowd. She also had the flexibility and strength to pull off a series of mandatory moves: one-armed pushups and the like. Where she was weak was in figure, in which women are judged on their physiques in roughly the same way men are in bodybuilding.

Here, the women were expected to possess, in a female sort of way, all the attributes celebrated in male bodybuilding, including muscle definition and the taper. It was a difficult look for women to possess with a weaker upper-body than men and a wider pelvis.

Those who had it often looked like men in bikinis.

At 5-foot-3, with powerful legs, Kelly Ryan had a gymnast's body, perfect for leaping, but lacking the upper body definition, including strong shoulders and arms, that would push her into the elite level of fitness competition. She also had a relatively thick waist, which meant that attaining that V-look taper would require even more work on her upper body than with other women.

"Because of gymnastics, she was extremely powerful," recalls Kephart. "She totally could do jumps that made the other girls look like they weren't even leaping the floor. I mean, she could go up in the air and she had a tremendous amount of power and explosion. But her upper torso was being overpowered by her legs. In fitness, you have to have a balanced look. Otherwise, if you go on stage, you look distorted. She worked extremely hard on trying to bring her upper body into alignment with her lower body."

That meant hitting the weights, while keeping her body as lean as possible. Kelly adopted a diet similar to that of male bodybuilders, high in protein and vegetables, low in carbohydrates, and sugar-free. For what the athletes call "good fat," she sipped olive oil and munched cashews and almonds.

At the same time, she maintained a strong cardiovascular system by teaching aerobics at World Gym and other gyms in the area. Her upper body grew while her body fat level remained small, no more than 10 percent, considered almost unattainable in a woman. By competition time, it would go down to 4 percent.

As she worked out, she let herself dream. Kelly had a realistic attitude about the fledgling sport of women's fitness, fully aware that even under the best circumstances her economic potential was limited. At its peak, the highest-paying competitions had prizes of $20,000, chump change in another sport.

Putting her education to work, the adman's daughter drafted plans to combine a fitness career while marketing herself, seeking out sponsors and playing up her personality and all-American good looks as much as her physical prowess. She had dreams of parlaying fitness titles into endorsement deals with Adidas and Reebok, retiring comfortably from the sport when her body inevitably couldn't keep up.

After months of hard training, she entered her first big competition, the inaugural NPC women's national fitness championships, held in the Imperial Ballroom of the Fairmont Hotel in Chicago, in August 1995. The promotion rules for the NPC's entry into women's fitness were lax: The top 10 would qualify for pro status in the International Federation of Bodybuilding, which was now sponsoring pro fitness competitions. The overall winner of the NPC championships got a direct ticket to what would become the Super Bowl of fitness, as it was with bodybuilding, the Olympia.

Kelly finished in the middle of the pack, fifteenth place out of thirty-five competitors. It wasn't good enough to get her a pro card, and it did nothing for her budding career. After one big competition, Kelly found herself at a crossroads.

Although dominant, the NPC and IFBB weren't the only players in women's fitness. A rival organization, called the Fitness America Pageant, lacked the pipeline to the magazines and supplement companies, but it did offer something the NPC did not: national television exposure.

ESPN broadcast Fitness America competitions, and Kelly decided to jump ship. The move put her at risk of being blackballed from the NPC/IFBB powerhouse, but TV proved to be too much of an allure.

And so, on November 16, 1995, she entered her first Fitness America Pageant, bringing the crowd to cheers with her "Popeye" routine, finishing with a solid sixth-place tie, and endearing herself to promoters and the ESPN producers.

In the audience, too, was the admiring Craig Titus, about to head off to a halfway house on a drug conviction.

If their initial meeting backstage after the show, when she hovered near her parents, made any impression on Kelly, it was never noted in her many interviews over the years, and Craig's halfway house and home confinement would ice his love life for the next year.

Kelly Ryan focused on her career, continuing to train hard, working on her upper body, and bringing even more razzle-dazzle to her routines. The toil paid dividends, and a year later, in November 1996, she took first place at the Fitness America Pageant Championships in Redondo Beach.

The victory established her as the first lady of fitness, attaining her goal set less than two years earlier out of college. She pocketed enough cash to live for a year, and got her face on ESPN 2.

But when the cheering died down, Kelly found that few people knew who she was. She got none of the other spoils: no photo shoots, no modeling contract, no endorsement deals.

She returned to South Carolina disillusioned and dejected.

"She won the nationals, and you wouldn't even have known it," recalls Kephart. "She knew that in order to get the recognition and the attention that was required to go to the Olympia level, she would have to be in California or Vegas or someplace where that was the mainstream. She wasn't gonna get anywhere in South Carolina."

She knew from her visits to Redondo Beach that out West was where the fitness industry was based, where the administrators were, where the magazine writers were, where many of the sponsors were.

With her pageant money she packed up and moved to Los Angeles to redirect her fitness career. She wanted to return to her former fitness organization, the amateur NPC, and try to earn her way into the professional ranks of the IFBB.

But it was going to take more than a change of address. The NPC wouldn't automatically take her back. Competing in Fitness America—and accepting prize money—disqualified her for a year from competing as an amateur in the NPC. She was told she could sit out for twelve months, regain her amateur status, then reapply to the NPC as if she had never won anything before.

She pondered her options. Fitness America officials called her in for a meeting, lavishing her with more promises. They said she could host her own television show called *Kelly's Girls*, in which she interviewed fitness contestants, according to Kelly.

In the end, she turned them down, telling them it was too little, too late, and set her sights on conquering the NPC. Kelly didn't compete at all in 1997. She hung out in Venice, training and socializing with other athletes, occasionally running into Craig Titus between his court dates—he had by now tested dirty for steroids.

After her year hiatus from competing, Kelly sent a letter to NPC President Jim Manion asking to be allowed back in. He agreed, for which Kelly was always grateful.

In an interview with Manion's son, J. M. Manion, a manager for fitness competitors who was reporting for AlluringFitness.com, she said: "I really thought that was the coolest thing your dad could've done for me. You know, he gave me a second chance."

Kelly re-entered amateur fitness on a modest stage, competing in a regional California show. She worried that the judges would hold her pro experience in the other organization against her and favor the women who had remained loyal to the NPC.

It didn't happen. Her fitness routine, now honed to perfection after years of work and top competition, propelled her to the title at the California show and set the stage for a bigger competition, the USA women's fitness competition in July 1997. A victory in the Las Vegas event would earn her a pro card and put her back in the upper echelons.

Going into this high-profile competition, Kelly felt she needed to improve her look. To win the physique round, she tried to emulate the body style of Monica Brant, a Texas-raised former bikini model with blond hair and bulging muscles, who had gotten her pro card in 1995 and was one of the sex symbols of fitness. Kelly thought the judges would be impressed with a fuller, rounder, Brant-like look rather than her lean dancer body.

She was wrong. After endless hours pumping up in the gym, Kelly finished a disappointing seventh place.

For the next competition, Kelly went back to a look more appropriate to her genetics, dropping eight tough pounds off an already fat-free body in just four weeks with constant, grueling cardio workouts on exercise machines. Working with a new nutritionist who shaped a diet for her pound-melting workouts, Kelly suddenly felt lighter and more energetic.

Flyin' Ryan was once again ready for take-off.

On August 14, 1998, she competed in the NPC Team Universe Nationals, and won it all.

She was now a fitness pro in the most prestigious organization, the IFBB.

"That day was one of the best days in my career," she later told MuscleMayhem.com, "because I knew what opportunities lay ahead of me if I worked hard enough to make them happen."

Over the next few months, Kelly Ryan finally enjoyed everything she couldn't get as a Fitness America competitor, from supplement endorsements to magazine covers, to an automatic pass to the biggest event in the industry: the orgy of muscles and skin known as the Olympia, in Las Vegas.

Meanwhile, Craig Titus bided his time in Lompoc. Just twenty-four hours after Kelly had gotten her pro card, he was sent off to federal prison for steroid use.

Soon their paths would meet.

CHAPTER SEVEN

CRAIG TITUS WOULD FONDLY RECALL THE FIRST time he saw Kelly Ryan after getting out of Lompoc. He placed the occasion as his birthday party in 1999, which he said had been organized by friends. If that were so, it was a delayed celebration, because Craig, born on January 14, didn't get sprung from prison until at least February 1998, with some reports saying it was as late as April.

But while the birthday party backdrop may have been a Titus-esque embellishment, nobody would ever doubt the depth of his emotions.

Ever since he had seen Kelly Ryan do her "Popeye" routine in 1995, he couldn't take his mind off her.

In between his various legal proceedings and incarcerations, while Kelly achieved fame first in Fitness America, then fought to return to the NPC, Craig would occasionally run into her at the gym. He would ask her for a date. She always refused.

"I could tell you absolutely why, as it was because of my reputation was that of a player, and she didn't want anything to do with me, because she was a good girl," Craig told Ron Avidan for Getbig.com. "I asked her out several times, she told me absolutely not."

So, at the birthday party, the newly liberated Craig Titus didn't just ask this time, he begged.

"Listen, let's just go out as friends," he recalls saying to her. "Hang out. If we like each other, cool. If not, then no hard feelings."

Kelly reluctantly agreed to be friends, but that was all.

"She was," Craig later said, "a hard cookie to crack."

Living again near Venice, the newly free Craig Titus plunged back into training to re-start a professional career stalled by prison. He'd lost a little size in prison, but gained it back—and more—quickly. Perhaps too quickly.

Craig would never be pinched again for steroids, but some wondered if he had gone back on the juice after Lompoc. He was not on probation—Craig said he'd opted to spend more time in prison rather than live on the outside and face the restrictions—so he was not subjected to random testing.

"He had kind of like a bloated, puffy look, something that's not hard-earned in the gym," recalls Shawn Ray, who had seen Craig at the June 26, 1999, World Pro Fitness Classic in Detroit, where Kelly Ryan was competing. "He might have been on something just to get his weight back up."

Sitting in the front row of the auditorium, Craig talked constantly about getting his pro career back to where he had left off. He complained he had lost two years of his life to prison and the court battles, and started telling people he was actually two years younger than he was, claiming to be 32 when he was really 34.

The other subject he couldn't stop talking about was Kelly Ryan, who would finish second in that competition as Craig and Shawn watched, her first since getting her pro card. She scored high on the 45-second compulsory routine of mandatory moves, even higher on her routine, but still lagged on physique.

Craig thought she was perfect on every level.

"I am going to go after this chick, she's hot," Craig told Shawn Ray.

Shawn didn't care—he had his eye on somebody else at the time.

"Go ahead, dude," replied Shawn, "do what you want to do."

Craig met Kelly at a party after the competition, and whatever he said then—combined with the begging after his birthday party—started to work.

After they returned to Venice, they dated.

It didn't take long in the gossipy world of bodybuilding for the word to get out about the new power couple.

Lonnie Teper recalls running into Craig that summer of 1999 in Santa Monica at a show Teper was emceeing. Teper had seen Craig with another woman at a show a few weeks earlier and asked him if that was his new girlfriend.

"No, no, no," Craig said. "I just started to date Kelly Ryan."

Teper did a double take.

By August 1999, Kelly Ryan was the princess of fitness. She'd followed up her World Pro Fitness Classic second-place finish in Michigan with a first-place showing at the Jan Tana Pro Fitness Classic in Roanoke,

Virginia, on July 17, 1999, and was now considered by many the favorite to capture that year's Olympia.

Craig Titus was an ex-felon.

"Everyone went kind of, 'Woa!'" recalls Teper. "Kelly was quiet, kind of respectful. It was like, Here we go again, one of these nice girls with the bad boys: Craig the womanizer, the convicted felon."

"Everybody was stunned," says bodybuilding journalist Ron Harris. "Craig had this reputation for going through women like crazy and having a temper and threatening people and being violent. And she had nothing but a really sparkling reputation as this nice, Southern girl. Everybody was freaking out about why they had gotten together."

With her new boyfriend, Kelly went to Las Vegas to compete in her first Olympia. The October 22, 1999, event offered the toughest challenge yet for her, on the biggest stage in the sport, and she finished a respectable second, ahead of Monica Brant and Susie Curry, but failing to topple Mary Yockey.

Afterwards, Kelly expressed satisfaction in her Olympia debut, and she quickly became the early favorite to win the next big event, the Fitness International, also known as the Arnold, named after Arnold Schwarzenegger, in Columbus, Ohio, in February 2000.

Kelly's primary challenge was keeping a clear head. After the Olympia she told AlluringFitness.com that the months since returning from her hiatus had been "surreal" and "crazy," like a roller coaster.

"It just seems like the whole year flew by so fast because I was on such a high," she said, adding that she was eager to compete in the Fitness International, feeling no undue pressure being the favorite. "I thrive on it. It pushes me to train really hard, and I love pressure situations, because it really keeps me on my toes."

She also had just scored a major endorsement deal with a supplement called Biochem. The manufacturer admired not just her beauty and athletic skill but her reputation as being, in her words, "a family-oriented type of girl." She hoped to use her college education to be more than just a spokesmodel for the company, but to take an active role with it after her competitive days finished.

Craig Titus, meanwhile, was finally making his comeback. On February 19, 2000, he competed in his first show after getting out of prison, the 2000 Iron Man Pro invitational at Redondo Beach. He finished in eighth place, a solid showing considering he had just re-entered the sport.

After the show, Craig met Kelly's father in the parking lot of the auditorium. Her father, Craig recalled, "could not stand me."

Still, Craig was in love with Kelly and told her father that he wanted to marry her.

"He said, 'Absolutely not, no way,'" Craig said in a Getbig.com interview.

DAYS LATER, KELLY COMPETED IN THE ARNOLD AT Veterans Memorial Auditorium in Columbus, Ohio, and finished first—the biggest victory of her pro career.

While still working on her father, Craig went out and bought an engagement ring.

"I finally talked him into it," Craig would recall.

On a spring night in 2000, Craig Titus proposed to Kelly Ryan over dinner at Del Frisco's, a steakhouse in Santa Monica.

"I cannot promise that we will never argue," he would later say he told her. "I cannot promise you that we will be happy every day of our lives. But I can promise you that I will love you until the day that I die."

It was corny, and it worked.

On June 6, 2000, Craig and Kelly married in Las Vegas at the Little White Chapel, his second marriage, her first.

They had barely finished saying "I do" when the bodybuilding community went into shock.

"It made no sense," says Ron Harris. "It was like she had been hypnotized or something."

It would become a favorite topic of conversation: what did Kelly Ryan see in Craig Titus?

She was queen and he was, at best, the sport's court jester.

His eighth-place finish in Redondo Beach got wiped out when he was disqualified for testing positive for diuretics. He had finished tenth at the Arnold, but was again disqualified for the same reason.

Among those with more than a passing curiosity in Kelly's choice of mate was Keith Kephart. Perhaps anticipating his reaction, Kelly sent her mentor a letter, saying there was a side to Craig Titus the world didn't know.

Wrote Kelly: "You'd really like him, coach."

THE REALITY WAS THAT, DESPITE HIS REPUTATION, Kelly was right: most did like Craig Titus. He would start fights, then call up to make amends. The magazine writers may have bristled at his temper, but they appreciated his quotes. In an industry that spent so much time on appearances and hype, Craig was refreshingly honest. And as people watched the Titus/Ryan marriage, they found a new reason to like Craig.

For all his machismo on stage, Craig never hesitated to let Kelly have as much attention as she needed and to step away from the spotlight whenever necessary, even as it increasingly shined on Kelly's career and not his own. At the same time, Kelly supported Craig's attempt at a comeback.

"Craig was Kelly's biggest fan and Kelly was Craig's biggest fan," recalls Dan Solomon, a former manager turned Internet radio host, who, with his wife, frequently socialized with Craig and Kelly. "They supported each other. And in fact, I would say it was one of the more endearing parts of their relationship. It was obvious: You would sit in a room with the two of them, that they supported each other in a way that was, you know, it was nice to see. And the more time you spent with them together, the more it became obvious why they are married, because they cared deeply about each other's success."

Craig said in an interview with Ron Avidan, "She is my best friend. She's the best thing that ever has happened to me."

They were still newlyweds when Craig proved just how far he would take his support for Kelly. When Lonnie Teper, in his column in *Iron Man* magazine, predicted Susie Curry would beat Kelly in the 2000

Olympia being staged just four months after their marriage, "Craig sent me this email calling me all kinds of names," Teper recalled.

Craig insisted that Teper had no idea what he was talking about and that everybody else was predicting Kelly would win. Teper challenged Craig to a bet: If Susie Curry won, Craig would apologize and concede Teper knew what he was doing. If Kelly won, Teper would apologize to Craig. So confident in his new wife, Craig agreed.

At the Olympia, the second of her career, Kelly Ryan finished second—behind Susie Curry, who would become her rival.

Afterwards, Teper approached Craig to collect on the bet. But there would be no apology or even acknowledgment that Teper's prediction was sound.

"All he said was that Kelly got ripped off," said Teper.

As was typical of Craig, he eventually settled down and "conceded Susie's win was justified, although I know he was just saying it to mend the fences with me," said Teper. "This was his wife, so you would expect anyone to be biased."

As Craig defended Kelly, his own career stalled, never reaching the moment he'd had in Redondo Beach when he got his pro card. In 2000, he finished tenth in the Arnold Classic, eighth in the Iron Man Pro invitational, eleventh in the Night of Champions and fifth in the Toronto Pro Invitational.

But the finishes didn't diminish Craig's notoriety in bodybuilding, and still earned him the occasional magazine cover. Part of his continued success was due to his marriage. But it was also partially due to Craig's realization that the part of his body that benefited most from excessive use was his mouth.

In 2001, having won only one major competition, Craig Titus emerged as one of the biggest names in bodybuilding when he engaged in a famous feud with another bodybuilder, a brash up-and-comer who called himself King Kamali.

Their back-and-forth provided hot copy for the magazines and set the Internet boards aflame—and made Craig, and to a lesser extent Kamali, the most sought-after men in the sport.

It all began in the months before the Iron Man Pro invitational, set to be held in February 2001.

By all accounts, Kamali had started it. In an interview for Lonnie Teper's column, the Iran-born muscleman declared that with his physique and crowd-appealing stage presence, he would be the man to beat at the Iron Man.

"I'm going to bust some people's asses," he said.

No matter that the king was but a peon in the industry, having never entered, much less won, a pro event. Kamali would later explain he wasn't boasting or disrespecting the more experienced competition; he was just being honest about his greatness.

Born Shahriar Kamali of Muslim parents in Tehran, he had been known as Shari when he moved to the United States and grew up in Virginia. Like many in the sport, he'd started as a wrestler, but soon found he enjoyed the workouts more than the matches, and turned to bodybuilding, When he was looking for a stage name, it was Jim Manion who suggested King.

Although a physical specimen, Kamali suffered from geography. Based in the East Coast, Kamali worried that he wouldn't get the same attention—and respect—as the bodybuilders in the West-based industry. Not wanting to move to LA and start working out at Gold's Gym with the powerbrokers, he found that he could make a name for himself by being outspoken.

The bodybuilding community went nuts. People showered Kamali with anonymous emails demanding to know just who he thought he was. Word began circulating that Kamali had even predicted his own victory, unheard of in a sport that got excited when somebody threw a backstage fit or called somebody a frog. Kamali responded that for the first time the bodybuilding industry was faced with somebody who not only could talk the talk, but walk the walk.

Among those who reacted the strongest was Craig Titus. He publicly countered that Kamali could not beat him. Craig even wagered $500 on it—a goodly sum for Kamali, who had yet to make any real money in bodybuilding. Kamali turned down the bet, but that didn't end it.

Thanks to Kamali's statements, anticipation—and spirits—ran high at the February 17, 2001, Iron Man, with fans rooting for their favorites.

One of the competitors, a legendary bodybuilder named Melvin Anthony, trash-talked with Kamali on stage, while the crowd went crazy. But it was all in fun, and the pair remained friends afterwards.

Then Craig took it to another level. Backstage, he taunted Kamali, calling him "big mouth."

Then when Kamali finished his grueling poses on stage, Craig heckled, "What is he, winded? Get up!"

Finally, during the crowd's favorite, the posing-to-music display, Craig called for the audio man to cut off the sound when Kamali went past the three-minute limit. Kamali portrayed this as ridiculous, since competitors routinely run long.

In the end, Kamali finished third against two of the industry's titans, Chris Cormier and Melvin Anthony. Craig finished a distant fifth.

No matter. The big winner was bodybuilding.

"The feud between Craig and Kamali was great," recalls Ron Avidan. "It was great hype for their first contest. Fortunately, they kept at it after the contest. They kept at it for years. They hated each other. They really hated each other."

It was never really clear why Craig took such offense at Kamali. In the pre-show hype, Kamali never singled out Craig; in fact, the fading—and aging—Craig was never considered a serious contender, which in the end may have been what most irked him.

On Getbig.com, Kamali summed it up this way: "He lost his mind at the Iron Man."

Perhaps, but the feud invigorated Craig's career. He transformed himself from a mere competitor to a bodybuilding personality.

He scored the August 2001 cover of *Flex*, despite finishing no higher than fifth up to that point, and continued to snare endorsement deals. Behind the scenes, he was a force in wife Kelly's career, advising her on everything from business deals to costume choices.

KELLY, MEANWHILE, ALSO WAS TRANSFORMING herself—in a way even more dramatic than Craig—as she fought to achieve number-one status.

It was while he was doing TV commentary with Kelly Ryan during the 2001 Olympia that Shawn Ray noticed something different about her.

"She very obviously had plastic surgery," said Shawn. "She had her eyes done, then she had her nose done. When she had her lips done, it was almost borderline Daffy Duck. She had a problem doing the commentating in 2001 because of her lips being freshly done. She had trouble talking. She told me she had spent about forty thousand dollars' worth of work."

From the start, women's fitness never could come to a consensus on what its competitors should look like. For some, the muscular women were objects of beauty; for others, they were mannish ghouls. Others favored the softer, sexier looks—hard-bodied chicks in bikinis—but who obviously didn't spend as much time in the gym as the bigger women.

Kelly's second-place finishes at the Olympia suggested that muscular was still at a premium. She kept the dancer's body, albeit a buff one, and continued to lose points to more muscular women.

At the same time, the major muscle magazines, which had been more than happy to feature Craig Titus as a cover boy even before he turned pro, would feature comely young swimsuit models as cover girls in favor of women who were excelling in the very endeavors to which the magazines were supposedly dedicated.

"You always think that if you win shows, they will put you on covers, and it just doesn't work out like that," Kelly once griped to MuscleMayhem.com. "So many times you will see girls who don't compete or are not even in shape on the covers of fitness magazines. I also dislike it when the magazines get fixated on certain girls when it comes to the swimsuit spread and lingerie issues. A lot of competitors get passed up for fitness models on these types of shoots."

At first, Kelly went with modest modifications, dying her hair blond from brunette at different points to get more magazine exposure. Then, observers in the sport said, she got plastic surgery on her face and body, trying to look sexier, more voluptuous.

From South Carolina, Keith Kephart watched the transformation with a certain sadness.

"I can't tell you the last time I read one of those Mickey Mouse magazines they put out. I don't read them. I don't care about them," Kephart said. "But I happened to read an article because it was about Kelly. And that's the only reason I read it: It was about Kelly. The guy who wrote it, he was right on target about what that industry had turned into: basically soft-porn promotion in magazines."

Kephart noted that the year that Kelly won the nationals, "She gets no photo shoots. But girls who didn't place in the top twenty are getting photo shoots. Hello! What's that about?" It opened up his eyes to the business, and made him feel for his onetime star pupil.

"When Kelly went to California, I was sad, because I loved working with Kelly. Kelly was ideal. She was, like I said, a great athlete, great attitude, great drive, all the things that you look for as a coach-athlete deal," he said. "But I'm so thankful today that I have nothing to do with that industry. Nothing."

Kelly's new appearance didn't help her competitively. In 2001, she got a second at the Fitness International. Although she won both the Jan Tana Pro Fitness Classic and the Pittsburgh Pro Fitness, she again faltered at the showcase event, the Olympia, finishing a disappointing third. This was the worst showing of her career, falling behind Susie Curry and Jennifer Worth.

Craig, meanwhile, did even worse at the 2001 Olympia, finishing twelfth, and again couldn't even beat Kamali, who was tenth in his first Olympia.

With each disappointing finish, Craig would complain about his situation and roar about Kelly's. The whispers in the sport were growing louder: Craig Titus was washed up; Kelly Ryan was slipping.

Craig's detractors feared that it was Craig bringing down Kelly, planting conspiracies in her ear, putting too much pressure on her, alienating the judges and the power players in the sport with his post-match outbursts.

Although not as outspoken as Craig, Kelly privately complained about the Olympia scoring, saying the judges seemed to be biased against her.

Shawn Ray, who also never won an Olympia in the men's bodybuilding division despite a stellar career, said, "She was always bridesmaid, and I think that stuck in her craw extremely. I know it did for me. The difference was, I didn't have people coming and putting poison in my ear about conspiracy theory, which I believe Craig was putting that in her head."

But there was something else that troubled people, something everybody talked about privately, that they worried might be playing a role in her career, but were loath to discuss on the record: Craig and Kelly's lifestyle.

Before Craig married Kelly, he was a self-described "player," known to party late and always have a girl—or two—with him. The hope was that Kelly would settle Craig down, bring some of her Southern values to the marriage.

Those hopes were often dashed.

CHAPTER EIGHT

THERE ARE DIFFERING ACCOUNTS OF WHEN MELISSA James first met Craig Titus. some say it was as early as 1996 or 1997, when Craig had ended his probation on his drug conviction and recently turned pro. Craig said it was closer to 1999, after he had gotten out of prison. Others say it was later, in 2001, when Craig had been married to Kelly for about a year and was deep into his feud with King Kamali.

Either way, most agree Craig entered Melissa's life when he visited her hometown of Panama City, Florida, while he was competing in a nearby bodybuilding show.

Craig would later say that Melissa initially worked for him as a driver. Melissa's mother, Maura James, who believes they met in 2001, says that a bodybuilding friend of Melissa's had introduced them and they were just friends. Craig seemed to make more of an impression on Melissa than on Maura.

"He was just another guy," says Maura. "I met him at Melissa's apartment, and she introduced him to me. He asked her to come to California."

Those were the magic words.

From a young age, Melissa James had always seemed destined for something bigger and better than Panama City, Florida, a Panhandle hamlet long on beach charm and short on opportunity.

A cute girl who would become a beautiful woman, Melissa was vivacious and ambitious, always looking for a way to turn her outsized dreams into a reality. By 2001, when she left for California at age 24, she had grown restless, adventuresome, reckless.

If it hadn't been a charming bodybuilder from California luring her to a life of glamour and excitement, it very well could have been somebody else eventually.

"Why did she go to California?" Maura says. "Just the fact that it was California. She had never been there. She thought she would like it. She thought that she would end up doing something really spectacular."

MELISSA WAS BORN ON MARCH 23, 1977, TO DENNIS James, a salesman at Tommy Thomas Chevrolet, and Maura James, a homemaker, and grew up with her older sister, April, to whom she was very close, and younger brother, Michael.

Rambunctious as a child, Melissa came home from elementary school one day with a flyer for a local dance studio. Only 7 years old, she pressed her parents to let her take lessons. When they saw her in her little tutu dancing in front of an audience for the first time at the Spring Festival of the Arts in Panama City, they knew she had talent, though they joked they didn't know where it came from. Neither of her parents had ever danced before.

As she grew up, Melissa expanded into jazz dancing, then hip-hop. She danced around the house and choreographed routines at her church. Because of her physical talents, a friend convinced her to play softball in junior high. But after a bad play, the coach yelled, "What's wrong with you? You look like a ballerina!"

He was right. After that, she stuck to dance, and the closest she got to sports again was joining the cheerleading squad at A. Crawford Mosley High School in Lynn Haven, a town adjacent to Panama City.

After graduating in 1994, she got a job out of the local want ads as dance instructor at Tony's Dance Studio. Before long, Melissa practically ran the place, planning the recitals, teaching the classes. Her business administration classes at Gulf Coast Community College convinced her that she could run her own studio.

At age 19, she opened Dance Unlimited. She secured her own business loan from the bank and found a building to rent. Her father helped install the mirrors, fixed the floors and put up the barre. She was the instructor, choreographer, and publicity manager, advertising the studio with fliers she made. For students who couldn't afford classes, she provided scholarships.

Now a beautiful young woman, with a lithe dancer's body, thick brown hair and blue eyes, Melissa dabbled in modeling and acting during the summer months, when business slowed at the dance studio. Her bikini-clad body graced a Panama City billboard for Alvin's Island, a swimwear shop. A family friend who owned two Xtreme Tan salons used her as a model in TV commercials on the local cable channel.

According to her family, she got jobs with Hawaiian

Tropic, Gotcha clothing and Calvin Klein, appeared on a Panama City television channel called Beach TV and once got a job in a commercial for MTV with VJ Jamie Kennedy. A friend who played on a nearby arena football team helped her get a one-season stint as a semi-professional cheerleader.

But the demands of the dance studio and outside jobs proved too much, and Melissa dropped out of college before getting a degree. Melissa also had been known to have an active social life and "had not been an angel by any means," her family later said in a statement to the media. But her partying—which some said included drinking and drug use—never got out of control, and she continued to run a successful dance studio.

She remained close to her mother, who had recently gotten a divorce and was now living in North Carolina, but visited Florida to see Melissa and her other two children. During these visits, Melissa spoke of being frustrated by the limited opportunities in Panama City, and considered moving to New York and trying out for the Rockettes, or going to California to meet celebrities.

It was around this time mid 2001—that Melissa decided to follow Craig Titus to California.

"She was impressed by the glitz and glamour of that type of world that was offered in Los Angeles," her family later wrote in the statement to journalists. "The parties, meeting the rich and the famous, the social crowds. But the family also thought and hoped that [Craig and Kelly] were a good influence on her. They were business people, a prominent couple in the industry."

Melissa did not cut her ties to Florida completely. She kept ownership of the dance studio, thinking she could leave it in the hands of trusted employees and make the major business decisions from California. It continued to operate, though not as smoothly as when Melissa was around, and just months after leaving for California, she came back to help stage the annual recital.

She was a different Melissa James from the woman her friends and family knew. She seemed tired and distracted, and people believed it was due to the stresses of organizing a recital from thousands of miles away. She snapped at people, which nobody had seen before. When asked if anything was wrong, she tried to put on a friendly face, saying she was happy in California. Melissa didn't say—and nobody seemed to know—what she did for a living in California. She said the arrangement with Craig and Kelly worked well and that the only time she was uncomfortable with the couple was when they were deep into training for competitions, when they tended to be moody and argumentative.

Even those who knew the couple well knew little about the woman with whom they were sometimes seen. "Melissa used to stay in the background," recalled Craig's longtime friend Matt Cline, in a Getbig.com interview. "She wasn't one of those people that you would know was around."

Craig would later describe Melissa as "our friend" and "one of my best friends," though some would later believe the tie was more intimate, her role with Craig and Kelly something more than just an employee's.

After Craig and Kelly married, they settled into an apartment in Venice, and soon rumors swept the bodybuilding community that they had turned their home into a swinger pad. By the time Melissa arrived in 2001, people would openly joke that Craig and Kelly were fond of three-way sex and wild drug parties.

"I heard the stories," says Lonnie Teper, "and I said to Craig one time, 'I hear all these stories about you and Kelly swinging. When am I going to be able to join in all this fun?' And he would kind of laugh. I remember I asked him directly one time, 'Everyone says that Kelly is with all these women.' And I was doing it tongue-in-cheek, laughing. I said, 'Is that true?' And he said, 'No, no, I want her to be, but she won't.'"

When Ron Avidan once asked Craig about his "wild and crazy" days, Craig said, "Every time somebody sees us with a new person, everybody wants to think that it is some kind of sexual escapade. I wish, but it is not. It used to bother us when we heard or read that, but now we laugh at it. We think it's funny."

Dan Solomon recalled: "Craig and Kelly liked to have a good time. There was no secret. And they would tell you the same thing. They enjoyed themselves. They lived a very free and fun lifestyle."

But pressed for details, Solomon hesitated.

"Yeah, how do I wanna go with this one?" he says. "Yeah, I don't think that I'm your guy for that, to be honest with you. I mean . . . and I could speculate all day. It's just no secret that Craig and Kelly, you know, had a good time and they enjoyed themselves and, you know, that's all I'm willing to say. To sit there and speculate on drug use and things like that—Did I ever do drugs with them? No. Was I ever invited to do drugs with them? No. Did we ever go into their bedroom?

No. So if you're asking me, I could not be any less qualified to give you anything useful in that regard."

Years after their Venice Beach days, a videotape surfaced. Shot in Craig and Kelly's apartment, one section of the tape featured the couple having sex. Another section featured a young woman, topless, getting a lapdance from another topless woman. In the background was the voice of Kelly, apparently talking on the phone.

One of the topless women was Melissa James.

Obviously, nothing about this had reached anybody in Melissa's world in Florida when she traveled home to put on the dance recital. All she said was that "things didn't work out in California," then told people not to worry, that she would be OK.

But after the recital, Melissa didn't return to California, as she had told some she would, instead staying in Panama City for several months.

Craig later offered an explanation for why Melissa left: Her drug use had gotten out of hand. Hooked on methamphetamine, she no longer was welcome in their home, he told the *Las Vegas Review-Journal*.

Said Craig, "I watched a human being disintegrate in front of my eyes."

With Craig already convicted of trafficking in narcotics and pinched for illegally using steroids, speculation ran high that he, and possibly Kelly, also abused drugs. Shawn Ray recalled driving Craig to the airport in Las Vegas after a guest-posing gig in early 2002, not long after the Olympia.

The two talked in the car about a fellow bodybuilder who couldn't kick an addiction to a drug called Nubain.

Prescribed as a painkiller, Nubain was commonly used—and abused—in bodybuilding. The drug would be injected into the body to improve fat burning, take the edge off the discomfort of dieting and to mask the pain from workouts. Highly effective—and addictive— Nubain was known as the crack of the gym.

As Shawn and Craig talked about this other body-builder, Craig confided that he, too, had been hooked on Nubain, but had kicked the habit, Shawn recalled.

Shawn then dropped Craig off at the airport and re-turned to the Las Vegas townhouse he had purchased as a second home—and where Craig was staying while he was in town for the posing event.

Shawn looked in the bathroom that Craig had been using. He found an empty Nubain bottle.

Shawn later confronted Craig, who said that he was just using that bottle to carry some growth hormone pills, and asked Shawn to throw it away.

Says Shawn, "I didn't believe that to be true for two seconds."

During the 2001 Olympia week, just months before the Nubain conversation in the car, Shawn had invited Craig to take part in his "muscle camp," an intense workout in which bodybuilders, serious and week-ender, can train with the biggest names in the industry.

"I felt Craig's excitement," said Ray. "Here was Craig, nose wide open, Kamali, nose wide open and all fired up. The next day we did my muscle camp, and Craig couldn't have been the more consummate profes-sional. He was at home, he was working with the guys, he was very friendly, and even though he didn't do well at the show, he seemed to have a grasp of why he didn't do well and was able to roll with it." With Craig's sliding career, he now appreciated any opportunity to get on stage, no matter how he did, Shawn felt.

Whatever his attitude toward drugs was, one thing was clear after those two trips to the Olympia and the guest-posing event: Craig was hooked on Vegas.

During that same trip to the airport in which they discussed Nubain, Shawn talked up the benefits of owning property in Vegas, telling him about his two-bedroom place for which he had only paid $91,000.

"Dude," Shawn said, "I'll show you where they are building some bad houses and they're cheap, too."

Shawn drove Craig about a mile away from his townhouse to a new development off Tropicana Avenue on the western edge of Las Vegas. At the time, 9539 Adobe Arch Court was nothing but a concrete slab in the desert, the outline of the Luxor Pyramid rising in the haze in the valley below.

When Craig got back to Venice, he discussed it with Kelly, and on February 6, 2002, they purchased the home on that lot on Adobe Arch Court. When built, it would be more than 3,000 square feet, two stories, with five bedrooms, three bathrooms, fireplace, pool, three-car garage and room for an office, all located on a quiet cul-de-sac in a brand-new neighborhood.

The centerpiece of their house was their custom gym, outfitted with black-framed equipment with red upholstery. They had the latest in body-sculpting gear, with machines by Apex, Powertec, Ivanko and Troy, from a shoulder press and lat pulldown, to professional quality dumbbells, 5 pounds to 200 pounds.

"The cost of living is low, the house is beautiful, and

there are not too many pro bodybuilders living out here," Craig later told Getbig.com. "We just wanted to get out of the scene, out of the public eye, and out of all the scrutiny and the backstabbing two-faced idiots that live in Venice. Venice is not a good place to live. It is full of jealousy and envy and people who would love to see you fail."

They didn't cut all their Venice ties. Melissa James rejoined the couple in Las Vegas, the first of at least two visits West, neither of which lasted. Melissa told her family that she worked for the couple, staffing booths at conventions in Vegas, meeting famous and interesting people, and helping Craig and Kelly promote their various products for which they had endorsement deals.

"It was just exciting for her," said Melissa's mother, Maura. "She didn't realize that it was leading to a road to nothing."

Melissa's changes of address took a toll on her dance studio. At its peak, the school had hundreds of students, but by late 2002, attendance had dwindled. She could no longer operate it from afar, and gave up the business. The college degree also got put on hold, permanently it turned out.

Melissa started talking now about going to school to learn massage therapy or going back into dance. She seemed to her family to be losing her focus, that drive that had her running her own business at just 19.

Matt Cline offered a darker picture of what had become of Melissa. He told Getbig.com that Melissa periodically came out to Vegas and fell into the drug and party scene.

"I tried to get her off the drugs a number of times,

but she kept going back to it," Matt told Ron Avidan. "She was addicted. She was doing crystal meth."

FOR CRAIG, MOVING TO LAS VEGAS SEEMED TO PRO-vide a new perspective, even modesty. In an interview with *Flex* magazine, Craig admitted, "I basically looked like crap at the 2001 Mr. Olympia, and I consider twelfth place a major gift now that I've taken a gander at the photos from the contest."

He said he had cut back too far on his water and "my muscles deflated like a punctured tire." But he vowed to return, better than ever, and "be able to finally beat Kamali," who he said had muscle structure that was "out of whack."

Craig said that if Kamali kept badmouthing him, "this thing is going to get physical, because there's only so much shit that I'm willing to take."

Kamali responded with the lowest of blows: "You can't have a decent rivalry with a guy you keep beating," he said.

The bodybuilding community tended to agree. By the next Olympia, both Titus and Kamali were non-factors. Ronnie Coleman won the 2002 contest again, and while Craig bettered Kamali, it was a battle for the bottom, with Craig finishing eleventh and Kamali coming in seventeenth.

In the women's fitness contest, Kelly again finished second, again behind Susie Curry. Kelly put on a happy face in her "Kelly Ryan's Corner" column, saying, "This year's Olympia Weekend was not only the most positive experience I have ever had at that particular show, but the most fulfilling. The Fitness Olympia, in my eyes, was a huge success this year."

Just as exciting for her, she said, was the Olympia's official after-party that she and Craig promoted, the beginning of what would become a lucrative side business for the couple, signing up sponsors and selling tickets for the bashes. "2,000 showed up at Club Utopia to dance the night away with their favorite athlete and fitness celebrity," she wrote.

CHAPTER NINE

IN EARLY 2003, WITH HIS CAREER SLIPPING, CRAIG made changes. Long affiliated with the Weider publications, Craig started writing a column called "Titus Talks" for Weider competitor *Muscular Development*, making him a colleague of columnist Lonnie Teper. Craig also picked up a new promotional contract, joining Melvin Anthony as a spokesman for Pinnacle nutrition products.

The new deal meant that Titus would be sharing cramped promo booth space with Anthony, with whom he'd had a tense relationship over the years, but he assured his sponsor that they had buried the hatchet.

After the Olympia, Craig set his sights on the Night of Champions, to be held in May 2003, working a new trainer who put on a high-intensity, twice-daily regimen called "blood volume training" that stressed multiple sets with medium weights rather than lifting the maximum. Craig's diet remained the same: high-protein, low-fat meals of salmon, chicken, tuna, shrimp—no red meat until closer to show day—along with almonds, peanut butter and cashews for fat, and then, when he loaded up on the carbs, raisins, honey, apple sauce and bananas.

And while Craig complained that magazines only wanted to hear him blast Kamali, he couldn't resist some digs, telling Getbig.com in the weeks before the Night of Champions that, "I am going to have Kamali beat before we even walk on stage. I will have him so upset backstage verbally that he will need to get a box of tissues before he even walks on stage."

Craig called himself "one of the few bodybuilders that had enough balls" to stand up to Kamali.

"I don't know about you, but I am not a spineless punk," Craig said. "He is a punk."

Then, after the show, "We are going to talk. We are going to go, man-to-man, face-to-face, and we are going to talk. I am putting an end to this. The guy is a big-mouth piece of crap, and that's it. I have had enough."

With that, he gave a preview of his climactic posing routine: pure power, from the muscular display to the music from AC/DC. "They will feel my wrath on stage," he told Ron Avidan.

Kamali wasn't so sure. He told *Flex* magazine (which had given him a new nickname, "Royal Pain") that his bad finish at the 2002 Olympia was due to personal issues—he had just broken up with his girlfriend—and "my mind wasn't in it."

But, he said, he was now in a new relationship, with a new focus, and he'd be disappointed with anything less than a victory at the Night of Champions. As for Craig Titus, "I'm so tired of that guy. I hereby knight Craig Titus Sir Jackass-a-Lot."

With the stage now set, the competitors appeared at the Night of Champions in New York, and this time the event nearly lived up to the hype.

In the May 31, 2003, event, Craig finished a solid third—ahead of fourth-place Kamali. Craig was undone by his stomach, which looked great in the early pre-judging rounds, but plopped out when he took the stage for the crowd, possibly because he had drunk too much water. But the story was the invigorated Kamali-Titus feud, spiced by Craig's comeback.

" 'Bad Boy' Craig Titus, showed up to do battle with EVERYBODY!" wrote Shawn Ray in an exclamation-point-laced column on Bodybuilding.com. "Craig wanted to serve notice he was not one to be pissed on whether it was on the Internet or by magazines!"

In the early rounds, Craig was "dry, hard and confident, all the necessary ingredients to pull an upset!" wrote Ray, but then ran into bad luck at the freestyle posing routine when his gut suddenly and weirdly fell out.

"A bit of stomach bloat stopped Craig in his tracks!" wrote Ray. "The contest being so close I believe Craig made some 'rookie mistakes' after prejudging that cost his runner-up spot! Possibly too many carbs, too much water, and heck I don't know? I do know if he came back at night as he was in prejudging he could have added a couple grand to his winnings and a runner up spot to his collection! He was gracious in 3rd place however."

The love didn't last the year, with a new feud breaking out, this one between Craig and the man who had just praised him, Shawn Ray. By now, Craig was filled with confidence, his third-place finish and edge over Kamali making him more outspoken than ever.

At issue were Shawn's efforts to become an official athlete representative in the IFBB, serving the interests of bodybuilders, who often didn't get all the spoils of the sport. Shawn needed ninety-eight signatures to make it as rep.

In the fall of 2003, shortly before the Olympia, Shawn rented a P.F. Chang's restaurant in Las Vegas and assembled all of the pro bodybuilders willing to approve Shawn as their rep. Shawn claims that among those on hand was Craig Titus. "Everyone signed it," says Shawn, "including Craig Titus."

The problem was that Shawn only asked for signatures. Nobody printed his name. Some of the scribbles were difficult to make out, opening the door for Craig to claim that he never signed that paper and therefore Shawn didn't become the athletes' rep.

Craig said he and Kelly didn't need a rep.

"Because of my personality and the way I am in this sport, and the way I manage Kelly and my careers," Craig later told Getbig.com, "for somebody saying they are going to represent the athletes was a little bizarre for me to swallow. Who does this guy think he is saying he is going to represent me when I have been doing it myself for a long time?"

Craig pushed for a panel of athletes who could more efficiently represent the bodybuilders, to prevent abuse and allow for better decision-making, than if only one person did it.

The dispute played out on the Internet until an athletes' meeting shortly before the Olympia, when a veteran bodybuilder from upstate New York named Bob Cicherillo got up to the microphone and implored Craig to "put this to bed once and for all."

According to Shawn, Craig came over, "relented," and signed the document, making Shawn the athletes' rep. Craig says he signed when Shawn agreed to his suggestion of an athletes' panel helping make decisions—a panel that included Craig.

"Me and Craig suddenly were friends again," Ray recalls, "until December of 2003, when the DEA started sniffing around our industry asking bodybuilders a bunch of questions."

Once again, steroids would be a factor in Craig's life.

CHAPTER TEN

SHAWN RAY AND HIS FATHER WERE PLAYING POOL IN his Southern California house one day late in 2003 when three federal agents showed up at the door wanting to talk. Shawn brought them into the house and they sat down.

The agents were from the Drug Enforcement Administration, conducting an investigation into steroids and bodybuilding. They asked him about the leading figures in bodybuilding: IFBB honcho Wayne DeMilia, publishing/promotions czar Joe Weider, Victor Conte, bodybuilding coach Milos Sarcev, several competitors, even Arnold Schwarzenegger, then California's newly elected governor.

Looking back, Ray says he added nothing to their probe. Although he still endorsed products and served as the athletes' representative, Shawn Ray was finished as a professional bodybuilder, retired, married, getting ready to start a family.

"I don't know what goes on behind people's closed doors, the same way they don't know what goes on behind mine," recalls Ray. "Some guys deal drugs, some guys take drugs. How would we know unless we were buddy-buddy? And none of us were. Here we are thrown together at bodybuilding shows and then we all go back to the four corners of the world."

Not everybody in bodybuilding believed him. Body building.com's anonymous columnist, IFBB Pro Undercover, reported, "Being that Shawn Ray was not served a subpoena and the agents possessed no warrant to enter his home, what exactly was the reason for Mr. Ray's cooperation? I would have loved to be a fly on the wall that day."

These were paranoid times in bodybuilding, as the government was delving deeper into steroid use in sports. The campaign had heated up in 1995 when professional baseball players were hauled before Congress, then exploded with revelations from the BALCO drug scandal that tainted San Francisco Giants slugger Barry Bonds.

In December 2003, the effort was just getting off the ground, as agents raided the home of Milos Sarcev, the bodybuilder who had trained world-class sprinter— and BALCO client—Tim Montgomery when he set the world record in the 100 meters in 2002. And now, in visiting Shawn Ray, it looked like the feds were searching for more bodies in bodybuilding.

And, so, tensions ran high March 5–7, 2004, at the Arnold Classic bodybuilding competition in Columbus, Ohio. Jay Cutler took his third straight Arnold title, winning by one point over Chris Cormier. Craig Titus finished sixth, and in the women's fitness competition, wife Kelly Ryan notched yet another second-place finish, this time being edged out by Adela Garcia-Friedmansky.

But the real drama played out behind the scenes, with federal agents subpoenaing at least five bodybuilders—some estimates ran to as high as twenty—to testify before a grand jury in Des Moines, Iowa, looking into illegal steroid trafficking in the bodybuilding industry.

Suddenly, this often unspoken element to the industry was now front and center. The central figure in the BALCO case, Victor Conte, was at the Arnold, plugging his ZMA mineral supplement. Even Schwarzenegger spoke out. Though he steered clear of steroid comments, he said the government should not regulate dietary supplements. "I have rarely seen the government do anything that was effective," said the new governor.

Among those receiving subpoenas was Craig Titus. The grand jury sessions two weeks later in Iowa were secret, and it wasn't known what Craig or the others had said. But it was clear how Craig felt when he got back to Las Vegas.

"He got even more vengeful and tried to point all the attention back towards me as being some kind of a rat," says Shawn Ray. "Well, to be a rat you have got to have information."

The anger, simmering on the websites and blogs, focused mostly on Shawn Ray. It erupted at the Orlando Pro Show in Florida, April 30–May 1, 2004. Accounts vary, but the clash between Craig and Shawn came at an athletes' meeting before the show, for which Shawn was the master of ceremonies.

According to *Flex* magazine's report, when Craig pressed Ray on what he'd told the federal agents, Shawn responded: "We talked about the convict in this room, like anybody cares."

Craig shot back, "This convict is about to break your fucking jaw! That's what he's about to do!"

Shawn Ray remembers it a little bit differently, with Craig asking him, "What kind of guy goes around talking to the DEA?"

"The only person that would be afraid of that, Craig, is a convict."

"You call me a convict one more time, I'll come break your jaw," Craig said.

Either way, no jaws got broken, and the competition went on, with Craig finishing seventh. In the end, the steroid scandal fizzled in bodybuilding, replaced by the shockwaves in baseball. No charges were ever filed against Craig Titus.

But the specter of drugs didn't leave Craig.

It surfaced again in 2003 when the spotlight turned on the late-night activities at parties thrown after competitions. By 2003, Craig's parties had become as much a part of the bodybuilding experience as the competition. Ron Harris brought his wife to Craig's party after the 2003 Olympia—Craig had not competed; at the women's event, Kelly got yet another second place, again falling to Susie Curry—in Las Vegas, and wrote a story about it for the magazine *Muscular Development*, which carried Craig's column.

Harris claimed that he saw drug use, sex on the dance floor, perhaps an attempted rape.

"It is nothing that I'm sure doesn't go on at clubs with young people or anywhere else, especially with professional athletes and stuff, there's a lot of hard partying that goes on after a contest," Harris recalls. "So I talked about drug use I saw going on, things that Craig wasn't happy about being discussed openly because he felt, for sponsors, it would present a problem for future parties."

Craig went ballistic.

On January 14, 2004, he posted this message on MuscleMayhem.com, according to Harris, who saved it:

I was shocked to see Ron Harris stating he saw someone having sex on the dance floor. Bullshit. I would have had a hundred people pulling me over to see such a thing. Never happened. I was appalled to read how a group of people were snorting coke.

Are you kidding me, if that actually happened it would have been a security issue immediately, I would have been notified as soon as it happened as I am notified about every aspect of every incident of the party because they are in fact, my production.

The fact is it never happened. You see I could care less about the write up; it's actually just bullshit, fantasy, tabloid, no big deal. But what the industry needs to realize is that Mr. Harris's fantasy writing may have fucked things for everyone next year because I can't even get House of Blues to call me back to book them for 2004.

I can promise you this, if I can't in fact book the House of Blues from this year, I'll make more from a lawsuit, that's a promise. Ron Harris and his J-Lo booty wife may as well plan on snorting their coke at other parties because they are officially banned from our productions.

Craig also complained to Ron Avidan at Getbig.com, saying in an interview that the article was "absolutely, no doubt, one hundred percent falsified bullshit." Craig said that if any of that happened—the sexual assault, the drugs—he would have known about it. "No one else saw it. He is the only one who saw it?" said Craig. "It is pretty much common sense that it was just a fabrication topped with bullshit to try and make a good writeup, which turned out to look trashy. Period."

Craig said that until a retraction was printed, Harris wouldn't be allowed into another one of his parties.

Avidan had attended the same party, even took pictures for his website, and didn't see what Harris had reported on. "They gave me full permission to take any pictures I wanted," said Avidan. "And I did. What I'm saying is, what he said happened, I didn't see that. It might have happened. I didn't see that and I was definitely there."

For Harris, Craig's reaction was reminiscent of the time Craig threatened to be at Harris' office in the mid-90s with a baseball bat and "use your imagination" after the 900-line report was posted about Craig's drug case. Now it was a lawsuit, not physical violence, but the threat left Harris rattled—and in a fix with his bosses at *Muscular Development*.

Harris would stick by his story, to a point. Harris later acknowledged that the couple having sex on the floor actually still had their clothes on, "dry humping" as Harris would later say. Although he declined to comment on what went on behind the scenes at the magazine, in the end Harris apologized profusely to Craig, and Craig also backed off.

"It was actually our mutual boss from *Muscular Development* that encouraged him to chill out about it as long as I apologized and clarified that they weren't having sex, they were just actually dry humping," said Harris. "Anyhow, I never wrote about a party again after that."

Nor did anybody else. Once scandalous, Craig's parties would begin to take on a worse reputation—that they were uncool—as post-event revelers found what they considered better bashes to attend. The coming months would pose the biggest challenges of Craig and Kelly's lives—and, some believed, marked the beginning of their decline.

CHAPTER ELEVEN

IT WAS SUPPOSED TO BE KELLY RYAN'S MOMENT, THE 2004 Fitness Olympia on October 29 in Las Vegas. With her rival, Susie Curry, now retired, Kelly had her best shot at her first victory since she first competed in 1999 in the biggest event in women's fitness. She was taking no chances this time.

Guided by Craig, Kelly trained hard in her home gym in the summer of 2004 and adhered to a grueling high-protein, no-fat diet. Always confident with her routine, she attacked her physique with new intensity, building her upper back and shoulders, creating what she later called "curves that I never had before," while at the same time reducing the size of her buttocks, the "curve to my glutes," to make her waist appear smaller and to attain the symmetry and taper that had always held her back before.

The fitness and bodybuilding community watched with great interest. As part of the build-up to the Olympia, Dan Solomon, writing for Bodybuilding.com, visited Craig and Kelly in Las Vegas, painting a portrait of a couple at the peak of their lives, enjoying a "marriage of strength" that had propelled them to the highest levels of the sport, with all the spoils.

Giving readers a tour of the couple's home, Solomon highlighted the state-of-the-art 400-square-foot gym featuring equipment with customized grips, the upstairs home office where the couple answered fan mail and signed business contracts, their media room filled with bodybuilding videos, and the backyard pool and Jacuzzi.

"Craig was quick to point out that his perimeter wall ensures complete privacy for those late-night dips in the Jacuzzi," Solomon wrote, "a healthy reminder that bodybuilding does take a back seat to certain things."

Zipping around Sin City in her new sporty red Jaguar, Kelly had become a fitness glamour girl, her toned, curvy body gracing the cover of the February 2004 *Iron Man* magazine's swimsuit issue wearing a barely-there pink two-piece while posing on the sand against a sunset.

Open the magazine, and the first things that hit the reader's eye are Craig Titus' shaved armpits, as he poses shirtless, arms raised, for a two-page ad in which he lauds the nutritional supplement Xenadrine for helping him "get in the best shape of my life" by burning fat and postponing fatigue.

While Kelly's buff bod graced several of the heavily airbrushed, glamour-style swimsuit shots inside the magazine, she still managed to maintain her credibility as an athlete. Echoing many pundits, Solomon wrote of Kelly on Bodybuilding.com: "Her stage presence is unmatched and her athleticism and strength are a genetic miracle. Despite popular opinion, Craig does not mind being second best in his own house. . . . These two athletes are business partners, training partners and best friends who also happen to share a bed."

Although Craig wasn't going to compete in the Olympia, he kept a celebrity profile, hooking up with Las Vegas resident Vince Neil of the rock group Motley Crue to help Neil get in shape for his new MTV show, *The Remaking of Vince Neil*. The partnership got Craig and Kelly front-row seats for Neil's concert on October 3 at the Palms casino-hotel. Calling the show "one of the best concerts I have ever had the privilege to see," Craig wrote in his "Titus Talks" column that "it was a great honor to train Vince and be part of such a positive production."

On October 29, 2004, a crowd of thousands, including Kelly's mentor, Keith Kephart, making the trip West to watch his former pupil, turned out for the women's fitness event at the Mandalay Bay.

When Kelly Ryan took to the stage with another acrobatic routine, the audience went wild for "Flyin' Ryan." She donned a fedora, plaid pants and a half-shirt exposing her rock-hard abs, and leaped, flipped, danced and one-arm-push-upped to Janet Jackson music, bringing the crowd to cheers. In the figure competition she seemed less self-assured, but the results of training were fully apparent, her every muscle rippling as she flexed in her teeny two-piece bikini.

Victory seemed assured.

At the awards ceremony, the announcer read the results. Ticking down the top five finishers, the announcer got to third place and said, "Kelly Ryan."

In her sparkly one-piece bathing suit and Lucite

high heels, Kelly froze. No smile, not the slightest attempt to appear gracious, her face locked in a scowl. She ran a finger across her teeth, rubbed her hands together as if to wash them of the mess and accepted her third-place medal and $8,000 prize, saying "Thank you" through a grimace.

There was a smattering of boos through the rest of the ceremony that rattled the announcer.

"All I do is read the names," he told the crowd.

After the competition, Kephart caught up with a still-shaken Kelly at a party, speaking to her briefly before he and his wife went to a performance of the Blue Man Group. The disappointment was all over her face—a face that Kephart believed had changed from the plastic surgery. Her body had morphed from the gymnast's physique he knew from the early days into something he didn't recognize.

She appeared exhausted.

Before Kephart could offer his condolences, Kelly apologized. She said she felt terrible that he had come so far only to see her finish third.

"I said, 'Don't worry about that,'" Kephart recalled. "I said, 'I was here to simply support you in what I felt might be your last competition.' And I did that. And that was the only reason I was there. So I served my purpose."

It was, Kephart recalled, vintage Ryan, thinking more of others than of herself. But people would be seeing less of it.

After each second- and third-place finish, Kelly would express her disappointment privately, but maintain a positive face for her fans. After her second-place finish to Susie Curry in 2003, for instance, the Weider-run *Flex* magazine was particularly harsh in its criticism of Kelly, taking aim at her strongest element, her routine.

But Kelly kept the high ground, writing in her online column that while "It really hurts when a writer destroys all the hard work you put into something with a quick flick of the pen," she'd spoken to the writer of the article, going through each element of her routine to show how difficult it was, earning a partial retraction.

"It definitely hurts my feelings, but at the same time, fires me up to prove that writer wrong the next time he/she sees me on stage," wrote Kelly. "I will use that write up, and the support of [fans] to help me prepare . . . I will not let this get me down; it will only make my next routine better."

This time, Kelly led her post-Olympia column with a ho-hum: "Well the Olympia Weekend has come and gone." She said she hoped everybody had had a good time, thanked her sponsors and congratulated the top-finishers and the winner. She made no reference to her own finish, offered no analysis of the show.

"Craig was really pissed when Kelly didn't do well," says Shawn Ray, who spoke to them both after the competition. "For Kelly, it was devastating. But it was more devastating because of who was telling her how much better she should have finished. I mean, Craig would stand up and yell at the judges when she didn't do well, while everybody else was cheering, and then you go home when that is over with and you get more of that, you become very resentful and bitter."

Added Dan Solomon, "The writing was on the wall

that her path to the top of the mountain clearly was being cut short, and it was obvious that she had become very frustrated. I don't think anybody would argue that Craig played a fairly large role in fueling Kelly's frustrations."

In an interview later with MuscleMayhem.com, Kelly finally aired this frustration. She noted that she had toiled to bring her physique into "what the fitness judging criteria requires," only to lose again.

"I am not complaining about this; I would just like to be able to understand it," she said. "People in the industry are brutally honest when it comes to comments about my body. Fans will come up to me and say things like 'you were a lot better at the last show, or you look better a bit fuller.' I would say that over the last two years people have consistently been coming up to me with very positive comments about the changes I have made, and I try to use the trend in comments to guide my progress. I feel that as a whole, people in the industry such as high-level trainers, diet gurus, and former competitors feel that I have improved dramatically but are not sure why I am placing so low."

Many agreed with her. "I would watch a show and I had Kelly in first place," said Ron Avidan, "and then when she would come in second, I would say, 'Did they see the same contest that I did?' But I'm not the judge. I don't know."

Predictably, Craig was outraged. "I realize I am married to Kelly Ryan and my opinion of her may be biased because of that fact," he wrote in his January 2004 installment of "Titus Talks," "but keep in mind there are individuals who believe Kelly has won the Olympia several times but will never say it to stay politically correct."

By the spring of 2005, Kelly Ryan was hinting at retirement, telling people she was thinking of opening a fitness studio in Las Vegas.

"Being married to Craig has been the best thing to ever happen for me in my life," she said. "He is my absolute soul mate and best friend, therefore we never clash when it comes to our careers, magazine exposure, or competing," she said. "Craig gets so involved in my shows. He even helps me pick out the themes and costumes of my routines. We make a killer team."

Craig also was slowing down. He bowed out of the March 2005 Arnold Classic "simply because the competition is extremely stiff," he wrote in "Titus Talks." "Believe me when I say that I was honored to receive my third invitation to the AC, but after analyzing the quality of athletes who just placed in the Olympia, I'm just not that confident I can break into the top five even though I placed sixth last year. One thing I've learned in this sport is you have to pick your shows strategically to continue to remain successful, and that's exactly what I intend to do."

Kelly did compete, and finished fourth.

Later that spring, Kelly Ryan was on stage again, this time as a performer, not a competitor. At the Contra Costa Bodybuilding, Fitness and Figure Championships, in May 2005, Kelly appeared with a dance troupe she'd formed, called the Vibe Tribe, whose members also included Tanji Johnson and Nicole Rollolazo, both fitness pros.

In her "Kelly Ryan's Corner" column, Kelly called the show a "huge success" and promoted the troupe's next appearance at the USA National Championships in Las Vegas the next month. "Plan to be seriously entertained!" she wrote.

After the Contra Costa show, Lonnie Teper ran into Craig and Kelly in the lobby where they were staffing a booth promoting various products.

"What's up?" Teper asked.

It was a more subdued scene than that described by Kelly in her column. Craig, now 39 years old, looked smaller.

"His career as an IFBB bodybuilder was over," said Teper. "He was never going to be more than what he was."

Kelly's dance routine set the audience on fire, but afterwards she had the aura of retirement. She had turned 33 and "now, instead of moving up, she was going backwards," recalled Teper. "I think the writing was on the wall. She was never going to win this dream of hers"—the Olympia.

That June, the Vibe Tribe did perform at the USAs. As the show's emcee, Teper introduced the dance act, and afterwards he spoke to Kelly. She thanked him for his enthusiastic intro and for helping get a picture of the troupe in his magazine. He recalled Kelly as warm and appreciative, the same old Kelly, but Teper had no sense that Kelly herself was going to compete again.

Something was changing in Kelly, including her appearance. Always proud of showing off her body, wearing tight, flesh-baring clothes, Kelly had taken to wearing long-sleeved shirts and pants.

At the same time, she seemed more focused on athletes other than herself. In addition to promoting the Vibe Tribe, Kelly took an interest in a woman named Mandy Polk, an aspiring fitness competitor from Germantown, Pennsylvania, who hooked up with Kelly through happenstance.

Mandy wanted to rent an expensive, custom-made one-piece competition suit that she knew belonged to Kelly. Mandy contacted the woman who made the suit, and she suggested getting in touch with Kelly directly.

"The woman who made the suit . . . told me that Kelly was having a hard time with her career in the fitness industry in general, and that some support would really be helpful," Mandy would later tell a grand jury, "and that she would more than likely . . . consent to renting the suit out to me if she heard from someone, you know, who had a positive view."

Mandy was that someone. "I really, really admired her," she said. "I really looked up to Kelly. She influenced me from the very beginning in . . . my interest of the sport and the way that I approached routine training."

Seeing Kelly's "willingness and ability to improve [in] every competition" inspired and motivated Mandy, who at the time was training for an August amateur competition.

Kelly quickly warmed to her eager admirer, giving her advice on everything from diet to mental preparation for competitions. "She would send me text messages that were, you know, motivating," recalled Mandy, "and she seemed to really want me to do well at my competition in August."

In 2005, Kelly also was working with another female athlete, a figure competitor—the term the industry uses for female bodybuilders—named Megan Pierson, a mortgage broker in her mid-20s who had followed Kelly's career for years. "I idolized her," she later said.

By chance, Megan ran into Kelly and Craig at a Baja Fresh restaurant across the street from Megan's office. They struck up a conversation. Megan had suffered a back injury four months earlier, and Kelly offered advice on rehabilitation and ways to begin training again.

Within months, Megan was at Kelly's house three times a week, working out in the home gym. By late 2005, the two women had become best friends. For her upcoming February 2006 wedding, Megan asked Kelly to be her matron of honor. Kelly gladly accepted.

But while Kelly was working with Mandy and Megan, she and Craig fell out of touch with many other people in the bodybuilding and fitness communities. Craig, especially, was uncharacteristically quiet in the spring of 2005. Rumors swept the industry that he had suffered a severe injury, though nobody could confirm it. He had not been responding to emails and his voice was strangely absent from the Internet boards.

Then, late in the summer or early fall of 2005, Shawn Ray got a phone call from Craig. Gone was the brash, combative Craig Titus who had once threatened to break Shawn's jaw.

"He called me out of the blue and said he was clean

and sober and was sorry about all the things he had said in the magazines about me," recalled Shawn. "He said he knew it wasn't true, but he was in a hostile place and the drugs were running his life."

Craig said he had just gotten out of rehab. He didn't say—and Shawn didn't ask—what drugs he was talking about or how long he had been abusing them, just that he had dealt with the problem. For Shawn, it was enough that he'd called and said the things he had. "It was really cool. He had found a new life," said Shawn.

Shawn invited Craig and Kelly to take part in a muscle camp in Dubai that December. He had already lined up several bodybuilder pros and was getting ready to print posters and advertise. Craig said sure—he and Kelly had attended them before with Shawn—and Kelly advertised her participation on her website.

In this phone conversation, Shawn believed Craig also didn't say anything about Kelly, even though people in the industry began to worry about her, too. Old friends faded from her life. Matt Cline, who promoted parties with Craig, moved from Las Vegas to the Boston area in July 2005, later telling Getbig.com that he wanted "to get away from all of the bullshit—from all of the drugs and all of the drama in the Vegas scene." Matt says Craig occasionally spoke to him by phone, asking him to invest in the new women's physique group and in the couple's Ice Gear store. Cline says he had the impression "Craig and Kelly were low on funds."

He also believed that well into 2005, Craig was still taking drugs. "Craig was telling me that lately he is

Craig and Kelly, shown here at the peak of their physiques and careers, pose with longtime friend Dan Solomon, who once admired the couple for what he called their "marriage of strength." *Photo courtesy Dan Solomon*

Ron Avidan, who runs the popular bodybuilding website Getbig.com, spoke to Craig just two days before Melissa's murder and says the bodybuilder was happy, upbeat and looking to the future. *Photo courtesy Michael Fleeman*

Anthony Gross told police that he rendezvoused with Craig and Kelly—who were driving the red Corvette—at this Shell station outside of Las Vegas before driving out to the desert, where the car was torched. Melissa's body was found in the trunk. *Photo courtesy Michael Fleeman*

Kelly was seen on surveillance video buying lighter fluid at this Wal-Mart near her house just before her Corvette was set on fire. The video also showed what looked like Craig in the parking lot. *Photo courtesy Michael Fleeman*

Kelly Ryan told police that she dropped off Melissa James at this Green Valley Grocery store near Ryan's house on the way to the airport—the last day anybody had heard from Melissa—but security video showed no signs of Kelly or Melissa. *Photo courtesy Michael Fleeman*

A trucker driving down this lonely stretch of desert highway early in the morning of Dec. 14, 2005, was the first to spot the fire just off the Sandy Valley Road turnoff. The firefighter who doused the blaze found the body in the Corvette's trunk area. *Photo courtesy Michael Fleeman*

Longtime bodybuilding competition emcee Lonnie Teper, here hosting an annual amateur contest in Pasadena, Ca., that he also organizes, had seen Craig's rage—and also his talent and charisma. *Photo courtesy Michael Fleeman*

A police search of Craig and Kelly's five-bedroom, two-story house with a custom gym—where Melissa was living downstairs—turned up signs that a Taser had been fired a day before Melissa was found dead. *Photo courtesy Michael Fleeman*

Melissa James as a kindergartner—her family said that she was a loving, rambunctious child who insisted on taking dance lessons when she was just seven years old. *Photo courtesy Maura James*

As a cheerleader at Crawford Mosley High School in Lynn Haven, on the coast on the Florida panhandle, Melissa James was pretty and outgoing, with dreams of runnng her own dance studio. *Photo courtesy Maura James*

As a teenager, Melissa opened her own dance studio and appeared in local Florida TV commercials, print ads and a billboard. She had followed Craig and Kelly to Los Angeles in hopes of a more glamorous life. *Photo courtesy Maura James*

Even after leaving Florida for Las Vegas, Melissa remained close to her mother, Maura James. Melissa had planned to spend Christmas 2005 with her mother—but she never showed up at the airport. *Photo courtesy Maura James*

Melissa, shown visiting the Jacksonville Zoo, returned to Florida several times after several attempts at making a new life in Los Angeles and Las Vegas with Craig and Kelly. At the time of her death, authorities found lethal levels of morphine in her body.
Photo courtesy Maura James

only getting messed up twice a month, but I have heard otherwise from other people." He said he didn't know if Kelly was using drugs.

KELLY SEEMED TO BE LOSING INTEREST IN COMPETING. in addition to working with the Vibe Tribe troupe, she had taken a greater interest in Mandy Polk's career, giving her pointers for preparing for the NPC Team Universe Fitness show August 5–6 in New York. Mandy finished a disappointing fifth—she needed to place in the top two slots to qualify for her pro card—and after the show, Mandy spoke to Kelly.

"She said that she thought that I would really turn professional at that show," recalled Mandy, according to her later grand jury testimony, "but because I didn't, she really wanted to help, to work with me, you know, one-on-one [on] my routine."

Kelly offered to give Mandy a one-week training session in her Las Vegas home, allowing Mandy to stay with her and Craig at first. If Mandy wanted to stay there longer, Kelly said she could rent a second house the couple had purchased.

"I said, 'Oh, absolutely,' " said Mandy, and she and her boyfriend, Ryan Chastain, made plans to go to Las Vegas.

Kelly also continued to give fitness advice in her on-line column, her tone upbeat, saying nothing of her disappointment at the Olympia. In the July/August article she gushed about her life. She said that she'd spent the weekend of July 10 guest-posing at an amateur show in Virginia and "had the most amazing time," the experience made all the better when she was presented with a birthday cake on stage and the crowd sang "Happy Birthday."

"WOW!" she wrote. "The whole experience blew me away and marked this year's celebration as one of the best ever in my life."

After recounting how her dance troupe performed at the USAs in August, and how wonderful that show was, she said: "My last announcement and news update for you avid readers is that Craig and I are opening up our first ever clothing store to launch our new clothing line called Ice Gear! We recently signed the lease papers and the store location is in the Village Square Shopping Center at the top of West Sahara Blvd and Fort Apache. With our Urban Styled workout wear, training gear and Sweat suits in the hottest styles and colors make sure you stray [sic] tuned for our grand opening!"

Guest-posing gigs and retail investments: Although Kelly didn't say it, people in the industry knew these were the signs of an exit strategy. They were earning money from their endorsement deals, real estate, Kelly's magazine column, bodybuilding/fitness camps and soon the clothing line and store. Their names still carried currency in the industry. It appeared they could make the break from professional sports much more smoothly and successfully than many pro athletes do.

What few realized was just how aggressively they'd break away—and how angry they were with the sport.

CHAPTER TWELVE

"YOU ARE LISTENING TO HISTORY IN THE MAKING," the announcer said. "Talk radio for bodybuilding has arrived. *Pro Bodybuilding Weekly* starts now."

At 8 p.m. Eastern time, on September 12, 2005, the show hit the net, the latest edition of a new online talk show, hosted by Dan Solomon and Bob Cicherillo, dedicated to bodybuilding and women's fitness.

"A big welcome to our worldwide listening audience, from Venice Beach to Las Vegas to New York City and London," Solomon said. "Bodybuilding fans throughout the world, we promise you another terrific show. I'm your host, Dan Solomon. We are broadcasting live. Talk radio for bodybuilding fans is off and running. Back with us for our twelfth episode of the incomparable and wildly entertaining, my co-host Bob Cicherillo."

"Dan, it's a pleasure to be back on the air," said Cicherillo.

When this edition went up, producers were still working out the technical kinks. Solomon broadcast from a South Florida studio, Cicherillo across the country from Los Angeles, and everything was relayed through a production facility. The show's guests would phone in from wherever they were. This resulted in a tinny tone to the mighty Cicherillo's voice, scratchy phone connections, occasional blips.

Carried by Bodybuilding.com, the show was the only one of its kind, bringing together competitors, promoters, the media and the fans. It had an informal, folksy tone. Cicherillo began by telling the audience he had spent his weekend in his hometown of Rochester, New York, for his father's birthday.

"And holler a little shout-out to my dad out there, just turned sixty-five."

Dan then asked Bob how the fans were reacting to their new show, and Bob said the fans "absolutely love the show." They said the original thirteen-show order had been extended to another thirteen shows and that they'd be broadcasting live from the upcoming Olympia in what Solomon called an "ESPN-style studio, and it's going to be the real deal."

They then revealed the night's guest.

"Bob," said Dan, "you know the question is: Is this show ready, and is our audience ready, for Craig Titus?"

"Well, I don't know if anybody is ever ready for Craig," said Cicherillo. "As anybody knows, Craig, he's very controversial, very outspoken, certainly not afraid to speak what's on his mind."

Bob noted, "The rumor mill is buzzing once again. Craig has been, candidly, uncharacteristically, I should say, very quiet, Dan. Nothing on the [Internet] boards, not many appearances. I ran into Craig myself at the USA. I know he was still coming back from an injury he had suffered before, but noticeably down in size."

"Well, you can call it the calm before the storm, and tonight may in fact be the storm," said Dan, "because Craig has promised to be incredibly honest and forth-coming."

After Dan and Bob talked shop, previewing the up-coming Olympia that promised to offer not just body-building competitions, but a Ms. Olympia expo and a guy attempting to bench-press 1,015 pounds—"which is absolutely sick, Dan," said Bob—and went to com-mercials, including an ad that Dan read for a Florida anti-aging center "where many of the top body-builders, fitness models and celebrities come for laser hair removal, aesthetic vein removal and body sculp-turing."

Then it was on to Craig as a guest, with Solomon ticking off Craig's professional accomplishments, al-luding to his legal problems, and mentioning his many magazine covers.

"But most would agree that Craig's greatest victory may have in fact been on the day he managed to con-vince Kelly Ryan to become his wife," said Dan. "Join-ing us live from his home in Las Vegas, they call him the Bad Boy of Bodybuilding, Craig Titus, welcome to the show."

Craig came on the air, his voice raspy.

"What is going on, guys?" he said, then answered his own question. "Radio talk show is a sport now?"

Dan paused.

"Craig," he said, "you know what, I'd love to make a

lot of small talk, but I know there's a lot of ground to cover, so we're going to get right into it."

He brought Craig through his bodybuilding history—Craig didn't correct him when Dan said he'd won the high school wrestling championship—and asked Craig why he loved bodybuilding so much. Craig called it a "passion" and said, "You know, you get hooked. If you get hooked, you are hooked. . . . It's either a hundred percent or nothing at all. You're in or you're out. And I just fell right into it a hundred percent."

Bob pressed Craig on his real age.

"Look, I'm thirty-nine," said Craig, who at the time was actually 40. "You can not say your real age in this sport. Everybody knows that. Since you're forty, there's some of the companies that think you're too old. They don't wanna do you. You know and I know that. . . . I'm thirty-four, actually. I gained four years yesterday. And it feels really good."

Craig discussed his years of legal woes—"My life was in absolute shambles. I made the fatal mistake of getting involved in helping some friends out with some steroids"—but expressed gratitude that bodybuilding had taken him back after prison without stigma. He said it felt good to have people bragging about beating him, a guy who "just got out of the can for three-and-a-half years."

He even thought the judges had treated him fairly—until recently. He blasted his sixth-place finish at the Iron Man seven months earlier, claiming, "I know for a fact that I was placed out of the top five because I am too opinionated. I opened my mouth too much about what they do to my wife or what they had done to my wife's career."

And he explained his seeming absence from the bodybuilding scene, saying that he had suffered a nasty infection in his calf that laid him up for more than three months and nearly cost him his leg.

"Fact is, they wanted to amputate my calf," said Craig. "They wanted to cut my leg off from the knee down. That's what the doctor told me, and I said 'You are out of your mind. Might as well shoot me in the head. I'm not doing that.' "

So, Craig said, he'd recovered in the hospital and at home, and was now feeling much better.

The medical report out of the way, the broadcast broke for commercials. After Dan responded to e-mails, Craig then moved on to the next subject.

And it would be a good one.

He and Kelly weren't going to just complain about the industry. They were going to do something about it.

They were creating their own league.

"Women's Physique International," Craig said proudly. "We are very, very excited about it. And Kelly's outcome in her last shows this last year is what really made my mind up to just go and do it, you know."

That was the Olympia, when she finished third.

Kelly and Craig were so angry at her perceived slight, they were going to take on the mighty NPC/IFBB and form a rival organization.

Listening to the radio show, Shawn Ray said to himself, "Craig is off his rocker."

The radio hosts were polite enough not to say so, but they clearly believed that this was a suicide mission.

Cicherillo reminded Craig that he wasn't the most popular guy in the industry, and that few might be willing to risk their own necks for a man who staked his reputation on being a rebellious outsider. Cicherillo knew this from his own scrape with Craig when Cicherillo held a meeting of bodybuilders years earlier in an attempt to start an athletes' union.

"You," Cicherillo reminded Craig on the air, "were one of the athletes who actually not only did not attend, but actually stayed not more than ten feet away from the room while we were having the meeting and refused to even participate. Now my question to you is this: Why at this point now would any athletes want to support you when you're actually on the other side of the coin now?"

"Because this has nothing to do with the male bodybuilders at all," Craig said, disgustedly. He called Cicherillo's efforts at creating the union "a waste of time." The top pros "aren't gonna do it" because they "have their money coming and feeling fat." He said he'd "felt bad" for those who'd attended the union meeting because "it really screwed their careers up."

Plowing ahead, Craig said his new organization wasn't a union, anyway. It was an organization of female athletes designed to give them a better way to compete, with fairer judges and more prize money.

Solomon pressed Craig on whether this new federation could go up against the mighty IFBB and NPC.

"Can you really compete with that?"

"Yeah, because there's plenty of women," said Craig. "There's plenty of women in the world that compete. I don't like the word *federation*. My organization that we're trying to launch, or that we did launch, or we're going to launch—it's a worldwide organization."

They asked what Kelly's role would be. Unspoken was that, despite Kelly's setback at the Olympia and signs she might be retiring, she still remained one of the best fitness competitors in the country, and had a few years left of a career. Also unspoken was a widespread feeling that Craig was dragging Kelly into this scheme.

"I mean, Kelly has talked about her retirement and me and her have talked about her retirement," said Craig. "And she's not really necessarily put an end to competing . . . because I think she's got a few more shows in her."

As for his own career, Craig said, "I've been offered a contract with another organization in Japan and Asia to compete over there next year, so that's where I'm going. . . . But this is no way saying we're retired. No, not at all."

"Craig," Cicherillo said, "obviously, you can't start an organization without money. And I know you've mentioned it. You have sponsors in place. Who would those sponsors be exactly?"

"Yeah, I can't disclose that yet," said Craig, "because we don't— I don't want anybody stepping in trying to— putting a stop to something before it's even started."

After a couple more questions about the new league, Solomon moved on, saying, "We're gonna move into a nice little treat, because when you get Craig, you get Kelly."

Kelly came on the line and started to talk.

"Hold up, Kelly," Dan interrupted. "Hold up, Kelly. I gotta pump you up real quick so you just have to give me another second."

He rattled off her list of accomplishments, all those No. 2s, "Not too shabby. . . . What's up, Kel?"

"Hey, hey. What's up?" Kelly said.

As taken aback as people were by Craig, they were absolutely frightened for Kelly. Her perky voice was marked by a serious rasp. "Thanks so much for the bragging. I appreciate that," she said. "You make me feel good."

"I love to make you feel good, Kelly," Dan said.

"Excuse me," Bob jumped in, "Craig's not far away, buddy."

"OK," said Kelly, "we'll leave you out of this circle. Go ahead."

"Kel," said Dan, getting right to the sore point, "you've won virtually everything there is to win in the world of pro fitness and you have a big fan base. Your résumé is sparkling. *But* there's one piece of hardware that is very, very blatantly omitted from your trophy case. Kelly, why haven't you won the Fitness Olympia?"

It was as if she were still on stage at the Olympia, stunned at her finish. Listeners were shocked at how bitter she was—this was not the Kelly Ryan of the Southern charm and cheerleader pep. She launched into a diatribe against the IFBB and its judges, namely the head judge, who had criticized Kelly's physique in an article in *Oxygen* magazine.

"She tore me apart in the magazine, saying that I would never win, you know, physique rounds . . ." said Kelly, "and my bone structure was wrong and that no matter how hard I train, because of the way the muscles tie in, that I would never be able to change my physique, so she basically made conclusive statements letting me know why the judges never saw the changes that I made to my physique, even though my routines would win every year. The judges did not see the changes."

Bob Cicherillo challenged Kelly, quoting from the *Oxygen* article and saying, "Now, in all candor, I mean, that sounds just more like a review of your physique. She doesn't say you're never going to win a round."

"Bob," Kelly shot back, "how about that I'm the only competitor mentioned in the entire article?"

"Sorry, guys, I got to step in," said Craig, and he noted that the judge quoted in the article was the head judge, so "the other judges think what she's thinking. You guys, it's so obvious."

"Yeah," Kelly said, "I mean, would you like to have your physique basically stated in a way that, you know, it can never improve no matter what?"

She noted that athletes could be fined $10,000 for criticizing judges. "So why all of a sudden, you know, would I not be upset about, you know, being spoken of? You should see the emails. You should see the number of emails that I got from people just saying that they thought it was tacky."

Dan tried to steer the show to another subject.

"I don't want to turn this into a vent session," he said. "You've done a lot of good things."

"No, no, I'm positive," said Kelly.

He asked her some general questions about fitness, and at one point Kelly drifted off the microphone.

"You're still on, Kelly," said Bob.

"Yeah, no, I'm on," she said. "I'm just talking to Craig at the same time."

Bob Cicherillo used that as an opening to ask about

the new women's fitness organization, pressing her on why she thought it would take off with limited exposure in the magazines.

She said it was only the Weider publications, and that other magazines were more open.

"I think people are just tired of being, you know, they're tired of seeing the sports being looked at in a negative way," she said. "A lot of the athletes are very unhappy. Everything needs to be moved into a more positive light. There's so much negative going on right now. And there's so many changes going on right now that aren't for the better that, you know, a lot of people are just willing to try something new. How about that? Try something new?"

After a few more questions, the interview ended.

Listeners were shocked.

Kelly had sounded just like Craig.

AFTER THE SHOW, CRAIG AND KELLY SEEMED TO drift further away from the industry. Dan Solomon said he probably spoke to them on the phone once or twice, exchanged a couple of emails, but would never see them again. His conversations with them were subdued.

"Given the shift in their professional choices, and given the outcome of some of the contests, there was no question that there was an obvious shift in the enthusiasm that you saw from Kelly," he said. "Kelly had gone from being a highly enthusiastic, highly positive, highly energized competitor to a somewhat skeptical, frustrated athlete who was wondering why she wasn't receiving the respect that she felt she deserved."

While Craig and Kelly blamed the industry, its politics, its judges, others blamed Craig.

"You know what, when you hang out with somebody like that, and become them, your personality will change," said Shawn Ray. "Kelly, towards the end, was not the same, happy person. She was miserable, it sounded like. Her voice did change and get husky and raspy, and she was one of those girls if she didn't like you, she would let you know. That transformation was five years in the works, but people change in five years."

Ron Harris said, "It was just that [Kelly] was so loyal to Craig, and Craig seemed like he was sliding more and more into that persona of a thug, and she was standing by him one hundred percent."

Kelly began talking to her friends about being "stressed out." While she wouldn't say why, many assumed it was because of problems with her career. Nobody seemed to know where the couple stood with their proposed fitness organization; after announcing its creation, Craig sent a press release saying he was no longer involved. Then he started telling people he was moving forward.

There also were rumblings that the couple were having troubles at home.

Craig's daughter, Ashley, who had lived with his parents, moved in with Craig and Kelly for a time in the spring or summer of 2005, several sources close to the couple said, but the arrangement didn't work out. Kelly argued with the girl, and this caused friction between Kelly and Craig, the sources said. Eventually, by the end of the summer, Ashley moved out.

The last hurrah for Craig and Kelly in the body-building industry came at the Olympia in October 2005. Neither Craig nor Kelly competed, but Craig was promoting one of his after-parties, this one at Seven, an upscale nightclub on the Las Vegas Strip. Few people showed up.

The after-party practice that Craig had pioneered had caught on, and now there were three parties in competition. The biggest was thrown by longtime bodybuilder Chris Cormier at The Venetian.

It was about 1:30 a.m. when Ron Harris got to Craig's party. Ron hadn't seen Craig in months; they had only spoken by phone. The first thing he noticed was how much smaller Craig had gotten. Harris felt Craig wasn't taking steroids anymore and didn't seem to have been training very hard. He was down to about 210 pounds, large for any other 5-foot-9 man, but 60 pounds lighter than his peak competition weight. Also, Craig was smoking. Ron had never known him to light a cigarette.

"He was happy to see me," Ron recalled. "I was with my wife, and we went in and shortly after, we saw Kelly."

As surprised as he was by Craig's appearance, Ron Harris was floored by the change he saw in Kelly, who just a month before had performed with her dance troupe and guest-posed at an amateur event.

She wore jeans and a denim jacket with long sleeves.

"Kelly didn't look good," said Ron. "She looked kind of haggard. I was just shocked at how much older she looked all the sudden. It seemed like she had aged at an accelerated rate since I had seen her last."

At one point, Craig invited Ron over to a quiet corner and started talking up the new women's pro organization he said he was still trying to organize, despite the conflicting messages.

"It seemed like they were on their way out of the industry completely," recalled Ron, "like they were just fading away fast."

Ron Avidan got to Craig's party even later, at 3:30 a.m., after hitting two other parties earlier. He, too, noticed that Kelly wasn't herself, but thought it could have been due to the hour.

"It was winding down. Kelly was about to leave. She was tired. Craig was tired, too. It was almost four in the morning. I was tired, too," said Avidan.

They chatted for a few minutes, mostly about how bad the party was.

"It wasn't great. It wasn't happening. It was weird," said Avidan.

AFTER YEARS OF INTENSE TRAINING AND TRAVEL all over the world for competitions and guest-posing gigs, Craig and Kelly's calendars were clear. Their last big commitment fizzled when one of the organizers of Shawn Ray's bodybuilding camp in Dubai had broken his back. The event—originally set for December 10–14—had to be canceled.

In October, around the time of the Olympia, Mandy Polk and her boyfriend arrived from Pennsylvania and moved into Craig and Kelly's rental house. Mandy began working out with Kelly in the home gym, but she noticed that Kelly's training trailed off. Soon, Kelly would stop working out, and Mandy no longer visited the house. The two women spoke only occasionally, by phone or text messaging.

Kelly's mortgage broker friend Megan Pierson continued to work out at Kelly's house three times a week, though Kelly's interests clearly lay elsewhere. With Megan's help, Kelly got a job—her first outside fitness in years—as a loan officer at Silver State Mortgage. Her website said, "Anyone interested in coming or relocating to Las Vegas to purchase real estate should contact Kelly immediately."

One of the couple's last links to the fitness and bodybuilding industry was their retail store. They had partnered with a friend, Gregory Ruiz, and found retail space in a shopping mall close to their home.

To help with the final arrangements, and to help manage the store, Craig and Kelly recruited their old friend Melissa James, now living again in Florida and working at a Gold's Gym. In October 2005, around the same time that Mandy Polk arrived in Vegas, Melissa moved into their downstairs guest room.

It would not take long for tensions to flare.

CHAPTER THIRTEEN

OVER THE YEARS, MELISSA'S ONLY COMPLAINTS about living and working with Craig Titus and Kelly Ryan came during those stretches when the couple trained for competitions. Their moods darkened, the bickering increased, and the tension would get so thick that Craig would check Melissa into a motel until the storm blew over and she could return, Melissa would tell her family.

There were also moments when Craig seemed to use Melissa to needle Kelly. He once gave Melissa money to get a manicure and pedicure, with instructions that she not tell Kelly because it would get her upset. Then later, when Kelly asked about Melissa's nails, Craig quickly said that he'd paid for it, setting off Kelly.

Still, Melissa never spoke to her family about the couple doing drugs. She said they took steroids, but that was it. She also never said she had a romantic relationship with Craig—or Kelly, for that matter—and she maintained a social life outside the couple's house, though the results were not always good.

She also never spoke of living in fear of Craig and

Kelly. For all their physical strength, the fighting was always limited to words. And as frustrated as she was with them, she always seemed to return, moving in with them, helping them with their business ventures, being their friend.

When she moved in with them in October 2005, Melissa told her friends and family that she was going to manage the couple's clothing store with plans of returning to college to get her degree. Melissa called home with what sounded like newfound excitement in her voice. She talked about placing clothing orders and meeting with the fire marshal to sign off on the store.

Megan Pierson, who saw Melissa in the home during Megan's workouts, thought Melissa was only going to stay in the house a few weeks until the clothing store got going. It was the usual odd arrangement, with Melissa being paid in food and lodging, but not given a salary.

Soon, Megan picked up on problems.

"Kelly did not like Melissa," Megan Pierson later told a grand jury. "There was something that happened in their past, and she did not like Melissa and she was very upset that she was at their house."

Megan had heard something about a falling-out between the couple and Melissa when Melissa lived with them in Venice, and that they hadn't spoken for a time. They then patched things up and, when she had problems with a boyfriend, Craig and Kelly invited her to stay with them, Megan said.

Melissa and Craig also clashed, Megan said.

"Melissa was actually very annoyed with Craig because he would demand a lot of her," Megan told the grand jury. "He would ask her to do one thing and five minutes later ask her to do another thing, and she would get very upset with him."

When Melissa called her mother one day, it was to say that she had attended a Thanksgiving dinner with Craig, Kelly and their business partners. The couple had started arguing again.

"Just the same old scenario: They were fighting all the time," said Maura James. And yet, "She never said she was in harm's way," said her mother.

Publicly, Kelly maintained a cheery outlook. In her November 2005 "Kelly Ryan's Corner" column, she wrote: "Hey everyone, I hope all of you enjoyed your Halloween parties and all the good tasting candy because now it is crunch time."

She made no mention that she had stopped working out for, perhaps, the first time since she was a child. She called that year's Olympia "quite different," not because she wasn't in it—she didn't approach that issue at all—but because the event had changed venues from the Mandalay Bay to the Orleans Hotel.

"A big congrats goes out to each of this years' winners and some newly crowned champions, all of your hard work and dedication paid off, and enjoy this coming year to celebrate and market yourself using the highly respected Olympia Champion title!" she wrote.

She said the big news that month was the grand opening of her clothing store, which she and Craig named Ice Gear & More. "We will be selling the amazing and creatively designed sportswear line of training gear, super chic cotton and velour sweat suits, silky-textured under garments for both men and women," she said. "Stay tuned to next month's column for updates on the grand opening of the US exclusive, Las Vegas Ice Gear & More store."

There would be no next column, and no grand opening.

CHAPTER FOURTEEN

RON AVIDAN WAS AT WORK THE EVENING OF MON-
day, December 12, 2005, at his desk at the health
products distribution company in Northridge when
Craig Titus sent him an email. Craig wanted to
talk about his efforts to start a women's fitness organization. Before Ron could email him back, Craig
called.

Sounding upbeat, enthusiastic, always the operator,
Craig wanted to tell Ron that despite the conflicting
reports, the plans remained alive. Craig said a Europe-
an group had signed on to help create the new organization.

Ron said that he'd be happy to interview Craig and
post an update on Getbig.com, but he needed to go
home where his tape recorder was hooked up to the
phone. Craig said he'd call him later in the week.

"That," Ron recalls, "never happened."

Two days later, Kelly Ryan's Jaguar was found in
flames, with a body in the trunk, and serious questions
needing to be answered.

◆ ◆ ◆

THE AUTOPSY ON THE BODY FOUND IN THE JAGUAR was conducted the day after police spoke to Craig Titus and Kelly Ryan.

Although both were certain the victim was Melissa James, the body that arrived at the Clark County Coroner's Office in a sealed bag, along with loose material, wires and other debris charred by the fire, was identified officially as Jane "Sandy Valley" Doe.

A technician opened the bag and marked the time: 8 a.m. on Thursday, December 15, 2005.

Little time would be wasted for this key part of the investigation. The stakes, always high when murder is involved, would be even more so in this situation. Although police had been able to keep a lid on the publicity, the apparent notoriety of the couple within their sport, along with the hints of a sex and drug scandal, were bound to make this a high-profile case.

From the condition of the remains, finding any meaningful information would be a challenge. The body was severely burned, as were the multiple layers of material attached to it. The blaze had wreaked such havoc on the body that it was initially difficult to tell what was clothing and what was Jaguar upholstery.

The pathologist on the case was Dr. Piotr Kubiczek, who'd attended the Medical School of Warsaw, Poland, served his residency at Ball Memorial Hospital in Muncie, Indiana, put in a fellowship at the Montgomery County Coroner's Office in Dayton, Ohio, and now autopsied bodies for the people of Clark County, Nevada.

Assisting the pathologist was technician Marnie Carter, a crime-scene analyst for Las Vegas Metro Police, who helped remove the material and would photograph each step, the grisly pictures some day to be shown to a jury.

The body before them was a Caucasian female, so severely burned that it would be difficult to tell even how tall she had been in life. Seventy percent of the left forearm and upper arm were burned, though enough skin remained that the pathologist could see the markings from two metal bracelets. Most of her right arm, both legs and, overall, about three-quarters of her body were charred.

The woman was dressed casually. She wore blue jeans—a patch of blue denim on her knee had survived the fire, as had some of the rivets. A portion of the waistband remained, located below the buttocks, suggesting that her pants had either been pulled down or never put on all the way. The front of the jeans had been burned away.

The woman was braless, her shirt a two-tone turquoise hooded sweater that was partially around her neck and torso and left arm. Traces of sweater material survived on her right side.

The pathologist and technician gingerly pulled the denim and sweater material off the body and placed them on a sterile sheet, where they were photographed.

The head and part of the upper chest were wrapped in layers of cloth, which also was severely charred.

Beneath the cloth was the victim's face—or what was left of it. The face was more badly burned than the back of the head.

But despite the charring, the skin displayed a strange pattern from something that had been pressed against it. The pathologist found that the imprint had come from the meshed backing of silver duct tape, pieces of which were found on the back of the head, away from the worst of the charring.

It appeared the duct tape had been wrapped around the woman's head, just above the eyebrows down to the chin, directly against the skin and hair. When the pathologist removed the scraps of tape from the places where the mouth and nose had been, he made a grim discovery: bodily fluids adhered to the backing.

"Her face, even underneath the duct tape, was baked," Dr. Kubiczek later told the grand jury. "It was not charred, but still, here was pretty significant thermal artifact, and this destroyed also her eyes."

Examining the neck, Dr. Kubiczek found evidence of a ligature: pieces from a cloth strip with an off-white, square-checkered pattern, in a tubular shape, circled her neck, compressing the sweater, with a clear half-knot or twist. The skin under the material was relatively well preserved, pink compared to the black that surrounded it.

Along with the cloth, there appeared to be a wire wrapped around her neck. An impression from the wire ran about five inches long.

There were also marks left by a metal necklace, which, along with other jewelry, had been removed and bagged at the scene.

Although discovery of the cloth and wire around the neck suggested the woman was strangled, determining an exact cause of death was hampered by the effect of the fire. The severe burns to the neck area destroyed

any possibility of seeing the petechiae, tiny hemor-
rhages in the skin that could be evidence of strangulation. The fire also obliterated any evidence of bruises
from blunt force trauma, as well as cuts and abrasions.

Examining the woman's internal organs, Dr. Kubiczek found from the remnants in her stomach that
her final meal had been chicken and rice, and that she
appeared to have been in good health, with no sign of
disease.

Looking at her lungs, he found them filled with fluid.
Edema of the lungs commonly signifies a drug overdose or serious drug intoxication, usually from opiates
like morphine or heroin. This also is a sign of a chemi-
cal injury, from inhaling something like deadly gas. Dr.
Kubiczek tended to believe this was a drug-induced
edema, of the sort he saw every day in the autopsy
room from drug overdose victims.

A toxicology test would later support his initial impression. The woman's blood contained high levels of
morphine and 6-monacetyl morphine, the ingredients
of heroin. The combination could mean the existence
of just heroin, or heroin combined with a dose of morphine. Either way, the concentrations were considered
highly toxic, possibly lethal. Also, a test of a hair sample found the presence of methamphetamine—a sign
of chronic use of the drug.

In coming up with a conclusion as to cause of death,
the pathologist couldn't decide among the many possibilities.

For instance, she could have died of asphyxiation—
lack of oxygen. By itself, the tape around her face

could have caused this, but she might already have been dead when the tape was put there. If she'd been alive when wrapped up, it would have been a slow, awful death: three or four minutes of struggling for air before passing out.

The opiate intoxication also could have killed her, though if she were a long-term drug abuser, as the meth in the hair suggested, the drug levels, toxic in other people, might not have been high enough to be fatal for her. He couldn't even say how the drugs had gotten in there—whether she'd taken them, or whether somebody had injected them, perhaps against her will. Because the body was so badly burned, it was impossible to look for needle marks.

If she had still somehow been alive when placed in the trunk, the fire alone could have killed her before asphyxiation by duct tape or drug overdose. The only thing Dr. Kubiczek could say for sure is that she hadn't suffered smoke inhalation. There was no soot in her lungs, either because she'd already been dead when the car was set on fire, or because the duct tape had prevented her from taking any breath, even a smoky one.

The bottom line from the autopsy was that there was no bottom line: it couldn't be determined whether she'd died from strangulation, drug overdose, fire or some combination of the three.

As for identification, the duct tape had protected some of the facial features from the fire. The length of the nose, size and position of the ears, position of the eyebrows, set of the eyes and shape of the head were consistent with the photo of Melissa James.

◆ ◆ ◆

MAURA JAMES NEEDED TO BE WITH SOMEBODY. SHE
called her older sister, Bonnie, who lived nearby, and
told her about Melissa's failure to arrive at the airport
and the phone call from the coroner.

Bonnie raced over and stayed the night with Maura.
The two sisters sat there for hours, with Maura staring
into space, her body wracked with a pain she had never
felt before, knowing in her heart that the body in a Las
Vegas morgue was her baby.

The next day, Thursday, December 15, Maura
packed her bags and went to Bonnie's house. Craig still
wasn't calling her back. She began now to worry about
him, and about his wife, Kelly. She worried that Craig
and Kelly were also dead, and that's why Craig wasn't
calling.

After she got to her sister's house, Maura got a call
back from authorities, not from the coroner, but from
the police. A man identifying himself as Detective
Dean O'Kelley of Las Vegas Metro homicide was on
the line asking questions about her daughter: what she
looked like, how long she had been in Vegas, where she
was staying, how she was making her living.

Maura answered as best she could, then asked the
detective about the body. He said it had been found in
the trunk of a car in the desert. Maura asked him if
they were sure it was Melissa. He said they thought it
was, but couldn't make a positive identification until
they found dental records. Maura couldn't help with
that: she didn't know of any dentist her daughter would
have seen in Vegas.

Maura repeated that Melissa had had that ballerina

tattoo on her lower back. She asked if they could identify her with that.

No, said the detective.

Maura asked why.

"Because of the condition of the body, ma'am," said O'Kelley.

Even in all her sickening grief, Maura had assumed that her daughter's body was intact, having been discovered in the trunk of a car. Perhaps, she now thought, it had been left on the side of the road in the desert. Visions of animals tearing apart the body haunted her.

Despite Maura's questions, the detective refused to elaborate on why they couldn't identify Melissa through the tattoo. Too early in the investigation, he said. He did say that a DNA test would likely have to be performed if no dental records surfaced. He told Maura to expect an express mail package containing a kit to collect a DNA sample from the inside of her mouth.

The detective changed the subject. He asked Maura about Craig Titus and Kelly Ryan. She knew little about them except that her daughter had worked for them off and on over the last four years, and most recently had been living with them as they prepared to open a clothing store that Melissa would run.

Maura couldn't remember everything the detective asked about Craig and Kelly, but she began to get the impression that he, or somebody with the police, had already spoken with them. Which means they were alive.

Which begged a troubling question: Why wasn't Craig calling her back?

◆ ◆ ◆

AFTER THE AUTOPSY, DETECTIVES TRIED TO RECON-
struct the activities of the key people involved in the
case—Craig, Kelly, Melissa and Anthony Gross—to
see how much truth lay in the accounts Craig and Kelly
had given during questioning.

Detectives went to the La Quinta Inn & Suites, a
two-story stucco motel with a tiled roof and rooms
starting at $80, five miles from the couple's house,
where, Craig said, Melissa had checked into on Tuesday night—and where he said he'd spent time with her
into the early morning hours of Wednesday, before returning home to Kelly.

According to the records, Craig had in fact rented
room #232 on Monday night, December 12, in his own
name, placing the charge on a credit card for one of his
businesses, Emperor Enterprises Inc. On the registration card, he put down his cell phone number and, for
the vehicle, his Dodge Viper truck.

From Melissa's cell phone records, obtained by an
administrative subpoena on Cingular wireless of West
Palm Beach, Florida, detectives found that she'd called
Craig's cell phone at 3:33 a.m. on Tuesday, which
would have been shortly after the time Craig said he'd
left her at the motel.

Melissa called Craig twice more later in the morning, at 11:06 a.m. and again at 11:19 a.m., the calls
coming about an hour after the time that Craig said he
had picked Melissa up and brought her back to the
house to resolve her differences with Kelly and to pack
up for the trip home.

The last call was the one to her mother. The records showed she'd phoned Maura James at 11:42 a.m. on Tuesday.

Using the cell phone number Craig left at the motel, police subpoenaed records from T-Mobile of Bellevue, Washington, finding the calls from Melissa's cell phone on Tuesday, but nothing else.

Another administrative subpoena was serviced on the records for the number that Craig had given to police—his business line.

This one turned up a flurry of calls Tuesday, beginning at 12:18 a.m. It was a call from his phone to Kelly—meaning Craig had called his wife during or shortly after the time that he said he was with Melissa at the motel.

Another thirteen calls were recorded between Craig and Kelly through the early morning hours of Tuesday, up to the last one at 1:41 p.m., about the time that Kelly said she'd started to take Melissa to the airport, dropping her off at the grocery instead.

Craig hadn't only been calling Melissa and his wife in the twenty-four hours before Melissa was killed. The records showed calls between Craig and Anthony Gross, the man Kelly said had gone with Craig to look for Melissa after the Jaguar disappeared early Wednesday morning.

At least five calls had been made between Craig and Anthony on Tuesday, the day that Melissa returned to the house from the motel. The first was at 3:28 p.m., the same time that Kelly claimed she had dropped off Melissa at the mini-mart on the way to the airport. The last one was at 8:02 p.m.—not long before the time that Craig and Kelly said they'd entertained Megan and her fiancé at their house.

More intriguing—and potentially incriminating—were the calls between Craig and Anthony the next morning. Craig had phoned Anthony three times between 2:31 a.m. and 3:22 a.m., before finally getting a call back from him at 4:20 a.m. Then there was a call from Craig's phone to Anthony's at 4:28 a.m.

That means Craig had been calling Anthony *before* the Jaguar was found missing. What's more, this last call to Anthony was at the exact same time he said he had text-messaged Melissa asking, "Where the fuck's my car?" He'd even shown the message to a detective with the time stamp of 4:28 a.m.

Was that text message really to Anthony and not Melissa? And why was Craig calling Anthony so early in the morning?

Had Craig and Kelly lied about the time they'd found the Jaguar missing?

If so, that could mean they'd had something to do with its disappearance—or Melissa's death.

Or they knew who did.

The calls strongly suggested that the couple had serious gaps in their stories—that a number of events had transpired that they weren't revealing.

Was murder one of them?

AT 9:30 P.M. ON FRIDAY, DECEMBER 16, DETECTIVE Dean O'Kelley's phone rang. a call was being transferred to him from a tipster, a woman who said she had information about a Jaguar and a body—and how Craig Titus and Kelly Ryan fit in.

O'Kelley listened with great interest, because up until now, no publicity about the case had been released.

The detective set up a time to talk with her. When he asked for her name, she would say only "Mandy."

CHAPTER FIFTEEN

THE WEEKEND OFFERED NO RELIEF FOR THE DETEC-
tives. Saturday, December 17, would be among the
busiest, and most fruitful, days of the investigation.

Police already had the recorded statements of Craig
and Kelly, the autopsy findings, the La Quinta Inn registration information and the cell phone records. Before following up on the call from the tipster known
only as Mandy, Detective O'Kelley started his day by
calling George and Angela Gross at their home to ask
about their son Anthony.

The detectives spoke to the mother, Angela, who
said Anthony wasn't there, but that she would try to
reach him. She called her son's cell phone and left a
message saying police wanted to talk to them. O'Kelley then asked what kind of vehicle Anthony drove.
Angela said her son had a 2003 charcoal gray pickup
registered in her name.

O'Kelley didn't tell Angela Gross everything he
knew about her son's possible role in Melissa James'
death. But she got the idea. The Gross family hired a
criminal defense lawyer.

After that, O'Kelley set aside time for the tipster. That afternoon, the woman came into the homicide office accompanied by her boyfriend. This time she gave her complete name: Lauren Amanda "Mandy" Polk, age 20, an amateur fitness athlete and friend of Kelly Ryan. The boyfriend's name was Ryan Chastain.

They said they lived in a rental house owned by Craig Titus and Kelly Ryan—and that they had information to share about what the couple had told them after the death of Melissa James.

At 3:54 p.m., O'Kelley turned on his tape recorder. Mandy Polk started talking in an account she and detectives later provided for a grand jury. Mandy gave her background, saying that she had come west from Pennsylvania to train with Kelly Ryan, whom she described as one of the biggest stars in women's fitness and an athlete for whom she had the greatest admiration.

Recounting her history with Kelly, Mandy described herself as an amateur fitness competitor and spoke of contacting a woman about getting a fitness outfit owned by Kelly, and how the woman had suggested she speak directly with Kelly, who had hit a rough stretch in her career and would welcome hearing from a fan. Mandy said that Kelly had first given her advice long-distance, then offered to train with her in Las Vegas if Mandy and her boyfriend moved out.

Mandy and Ryan had taken Kelly up on her offer and arrived in Las Vegas in October, around the time of the Fitness Olympia. Mandy worked out with Kelly in her home gym, regularly at first, then less frequently. After the Olympia, Kelly's own workout regime lessened, and she stopped training altogether in late November and early December. After that, they'd communicated via phone calls or text messages, except for a day in early December when Kelly had gone to the rental house to talk about fitness and look at Mandy's contest pictures.

The next time Mandy heard from Kelly was about a week later, on Thursday, December 15—the day after the body was discovered and the couple were interviewed, the detective noted—when she'd received a phone call. The name Craig Titus popped up on her cell phone's caller ID.

That surprised her; she never got calls from Craig, only Kelly. When Mandy answered, she recognized Craig's gravelly voice.

Craig said he and Kelly were coming over to the rental house later that day because they had "run into some trouble," according to Mandy.

Mandy asked him what it was. He said it was a long story, difficult to explain on the phone, but the bottom line was that he and Kelly were planning to leave town—for a long time.

Mandy was struck by the fact that Craig didn't ask if they could come over. He announced it.

"Just make sure you call before you come, if you don't mind," Mandy told him.

"Oh, sure, honey," said Craig, "we'll be calling you around six o'clock."

Instead, Craig and Kelly arrived about an hour earlier than that, at 5, with their dog Joey. They'd never called ahead; they'd just shown up. It wasn't clear how they'd gotten there—they had no car that Mandy could see.

Mandy was upstairs taking a nap when the knock came on the door. Her boyfriend Ryan let the couple in.

Immediately, Kelly went up the stairs. Mandy intended to change clothes, but before she could, Kelly embraced her outside her bedroom.

Sobbing, Kelly seemed to be in a panic.

"Oh, my God, the police found my car burned up with a body in it," Kelly blurted, according to Mandy.

At first, Mandy didn't say anything. She was confused.

"What happened?" Mandy asked.

Kelly didn't answer. Instead, she said, "Homicide was at our house this morning." (In fact, police had been there the day before.) "There's a dead body in my car and it was burned up in the desert."

Asked again what was going on, Kelly explained that her roommate was missing and that police said the body was that of the roommate, who'd probably stolen the car.

"I didn't know you had a roommate," said Mandy.

In all the time she had spent with Kelly, she'd never heard the name Melissa James or seen anybody at the home who might have been her, Mandy told the detective.

As the women spoke, Mandy said, Craig paced around the house downstairs checking the doors and closing the blinds.

Mandy went inside her room to change while Kelly remained outside the door. Now it was Mandy's turn to panic. She felt confused and concerned for her mentor.

When she had changed, she spoke again to Kelly, asking for more information. But Craig came upstairs and interrupted.

"The less you know, the better," he told Mandy. "Really, we don't want to involve you guys."

All he would say about the dead woman was that "She was a drug addict and stealing from us."

"She was a drug addict?" Mandy asked.

"Yeah," said Kelly, "she was a meth addict. She was a fucking tweeker."

Now the couple were saying all sorts of strange things, blurting out details, and Mandy struggled to follow them.

This drug addict, Melissa, had been in their care. They had taken her in to help her out. They'd let her use the red Jaguar when Kelly didn't need it. They were trying to give her her own space in the house, a sense of having her own life and freedom to come and go. But she was stealing from them, trying to take their identities, may even have tried to kill them by poisoning their drinking glasses.

They said the car, the Jaguar that Melissa had been allowed to use, was in the driveway one minute, and the next it was gone. And so was Melissa.

And then, they said, homicide detectives came over to ask about the car.

"Did you notice that the car was gone? Did you hear anything?" Mandy asked.

They said they hadn't heard anything because they had been upstairs.

Pressed for more details about the missing Melissa, Kelly told Mandy that Melissa was supposed to have flown out of town the evening before. She said she'd helped Melissa pack and that someone had driven

Melissa off, and then the next thing they knew she was found dead in the Jaguar.

The story was beyond strange. And so was the couple's demeanor as described by Mandy. About an hour after arriving at the rental house, Craig said he was hungry. He wanted Chinese food and, he said, "the girls" should get it.

Kelly and Mandy drove Mandy's car, leaving at about 7 p.m.

At first, Kelly rambled about this Melissa—how Melissa had been a drug user with erratic behavior, unreliable and strange. Kelly felt stressed out having a person like this in her home.

"We had talked several times," Mandy told Kelly, "and you had said that you were stressed out. You never ever said anything about the roommate being the source of your stress or that she was bothering you. So what's up with that?"

"You know, Mandy, when things happen and something is going on in your life that causes you problems or creates a stressful situation, it isn't easy to always pinpoint what it is," Kelly said. "I think Melissa was an example of that to me."

"Fair enough," said Mandy.

But it didn't clear things up. Mandy still tried to figure out how it was that Melissa had ended up dead in a burning car.

Kelly and Craig had said that Melissa was not even supposed to be in Nevada the morning she died; she had planned to fly out of town the night before. Melissa had left the house at 2 p.m. for the airport. The details flew, and Mandy struggled to put them together.

Mandy asked what time the flight was. Kelly couldn't say: it was supposed to leave at 10 p.m. or maybe it was supposed to arrive at 10 p.m. She couldn't recall.

So why had she left the house at 2 p.m.? asked Mandy.

Kelly said she didn't know.

Suddenly, as they drove, Kelly seemed frazzled, more panicked than ever, like she was holding something back.

"OK, Mandy, I can't lie to you anymore," she finally said. "I found the girl dead in her room of a drug overdose."

Mandy paused.

"Oh, my gosh. Wow," was all she could say. "So you burned her body up in your car?"

"Yeah," Kelly said.

Mandy was aghast. She didn't know what to think now.

Why, she asked Kelly, didn't she just call 911 when she found Melissa dead, since it was obviously not her fault?

"Why," Mandy asked, "would you destroy the evidence of that—because then that just incriminates you?"

"I'm fucked," Kelly said. "I bought seven bottles of lighter fluid with my credit card at Wal-Mart."

The story was getting more bizarre by the moment.

Kelly said that after finding Melissa dead, she had freaked out. She and Craig decided it was best to get rid of the body. If the press found out about this, Kelly was sunk. She was trying to move forward with her career, which she felt had already slipped. This would just make it worse.

Kelly told Mandy that Craig had come up with a plan. He told Kelly, "No body, no crime."

So they went out to the desert and set fire to the car.

By now Mandy and Kelly had arrived at the restaurant, and they got the food. Kelly said she was going to go next door to Cold Stone Creamery for ice cream for dessert. She asked if Mandy wanted some. She said no, that she'd just wait in the car.

On the way back to the house, Mandy asked, "So you found the body in her room?"

Yes, said Kelly, in Melissa's room, not theirs.

When they returned to the rental house, they brought the food upstairs, because Craig didn't want to be near the windows downstairs. Mandy brought plates and silverware up.

"I'm going to go in my car and get your drinks," Mandy told Kelly, referring to the Cokes and Diet Cokes in the car. "You and Craig can start eating upstairs."

It was the first moment that Mandy had had away from Kelly. She pulled her boyfriend Ryan into the garage.

"Kelly told me that they burned the roommate in the car," she quickly told him. "Kelly said they found her dead of a drug overdose. But she doesn't want anyone—Craig or you—to know that she told."

There wasn't time to figure out what to do. Mandy got the drinks from the car and went back upstairs.

They all ate dinner. It was a long, tense evening. Craig and Kelly asked if they could spend the night; Mandy and Ryan reluctantly agreed. Craig said it was probably only for a night, that the couple were planning on leaving soon, anyway, looking to bolt to Europe, Greece or Mexico, or some country with a non-extradition policy.

At one point in the evening, Mandy excused herself and went to Albertson's grocery store to buy crackers for Craig and Kelly's dog. She was so confused, feeling alone and scared, that she thought about not returning. But she did. She went to her bedroom and got ready for bed.

Kelly was in the bathroom, washing her tired face.

Kelly said she was nervous and afraid. "I can't have my name attached to a murder," she told Mandy. "I didn't kill anyone. Whether Craig did it or had someone take care of it, I don't know. All I know is that I didn't kill anyone."

Mandy shuddered. She realized that for the first time that night, Kelly had used the word *murder*.

That night, Kelly and Craig were so paranoid, they slept on the floor in Mandy and Ryan's room, away from the windows. Mandy offered them the bed, but they refused. Mandy stayed in the room with them, struggling to sleep. Ryan didn't sleep at all. He worked in a nightclub and was used to staying up all night. He watched a movie in the hallway.

Mandy awoke Friday morning, December 16, to find Craig and Kelly on their phones making plans. Mandy believed Craig was speaking to his attorney, and also seemed to be calling a friend who appeared to be refusing to let him stay at their house.

This seemed to get Craig upset.

All Mandy wanted was for them to leave.

Finally she got her wish. Craig and Kelly asked if Mandy could drive them to a nearby La Quinta Inn. Mandy said yes, but Ryan came with them. They got to the motel, which was located on West Sahara.

The detective noted this was the same motel where Craig had taken Melissa at the beginning of that week.

The motel required a credit card. Mandy recalled that Craig didn't want to put the room in his name and asked Ryan if he would take care of it. Ryan refused.

They got back into the car and went to another motel, a Holiday Inn, which would accept cash. Ryan filled out the registration form while the other three stayed in the car, Craig still smoldering because Ryan wouldn't put the room in his name back at the La Quinta.

"I'm just not like that. I'm not like that with friends," Mandy overheard Craig telling Kelly. "I'll go all out. It doesn't matter who they are or what happened."

"Well," interjected Mandy, "you have to understand his position. He doesn't even know what he's involved with here, and you're involving him by saying that you need him to get you a room."

When Ryan returned with the room key, Craig and Kelly left the car, and a relieved Mandy and Ryan drove home.

Later that evening, curiosity overcame Mandy Polk and she called Kelly's cell phone. Mandy felt like there had to be more to know, that this wasn't everything, she needed to hear more from the woman who had so inspired her. But Kelly wouldn't talk about it anymore.

The two women would never speak again.

Four hours later, Mandy called the police department, giving only her first name.

THE SAME SATURDAY THAT MANDY WAS BEING IN-terviewed, Melissa James' mother, Maura, got the call she'd been waiting for since her daughter had failed to show up at the airport.

Since Wednesday, Maura had repeatedly phoned Craig Titus, leaving several messages on his voice mail. She'd first called within hours after going to the airport.

She called him again the next day, after speaking with the Las Vegas homicide detective who had asked Maura about the last time she had seen her daughter. Again, Craig didn't answer his cell phone, and she left a message.

She called him yet again on Friday, and again left a message.

Finally, on Saturday, her cell phone rang.

"This is Craig," he said, explaining he hadn't returned her calls because he was out of town and didn't have that particular phone with him.

According to Maura's account of the conversation, Craig sounded smug and confident, saying he had purchased an airline ticket for Melissa to fly home the night of December 13 and that he hadn't seen her since. He said the police had spoken to him about finding a dead woman in the trunk of Kelly's Jaguar.

But Craig insisted he'd had nothing to do with the situation. In fact, he said he didn't believe the victim was Melissa, and told her mother he believed Melissa was a thief who'd staged the whole thing to get a new identity.

Craig added that Maura James needn't worry—he wasn't mad at Melissa, because the insurance would reimburse him for the car. What's more, he said, he had spoken to a man who claimed to have seen her the day the body was found.

Craig gave Maura the man's phone number.

Now she didn't know what to think. Maura had spoken to the coroner's office and a homicide detective that week. They seemed sure the body was Melissa's. Maura told Craig that police planned to do DNA testing on the body to determine the identity.

"Really?" Craig said. Maura thought she could hear the confidence leaving his voice.

But Craig had given her a glimmer of hope that Melissa was alive. After talking to Craig, Maura called the man who supposedly saw Melissa. He said he had been out of town all week and didn't know what she was talking about.

The glimmer went out immediately.

CHAPTER SIXTEEN

BY MONDAY, DECEMBER 19, 2005, FIVE DAYS AFTER
the burning car had been found, police heard back
from the newly hired lawyer for Anthony Gross. The
attorney, Louis Palazzo, said Anthony would talk.

At 6 p.m., detectives Dean O'Kelley and Robert
Wilson arrived at the Fourth Street law office, where
they found Anthony Gross and his counsel. Over the
next forty-five minutes, Gross provided a taped statement about his activities the morning the burning car
had been found. Details in that statement were later revealed in a grand jury testimony and a police affidavit.

His cell phone, Anthony told the detectives, had
started ringing at about 3 a.m. that Tuesday morning,
while he was still asleep at his girlfriend's house. He'd
ignored the first couple of calls and instead cuddled in
bed with his girlfriend.

Eventually, he checked the call log and saw that the
calls had come from his friend Craig Titus. The two had
spoken the night before, he told the detectives, around 8
or 9 p.m. This jibed with phone records showing a call
between them at 8:08 p.m. on Tuesday, December 13.

When Anthony finally spoke to Craig that Wednesday morning, Craig told him they needed to meet—Craig wanted Anthony to help him get gasoline.

Anthony got out of bed. Still wearing his pajama bottoms, he drove to a Shell station on the corner of Fort Apache Road and Blue Diamond Highway, which becomes state Route 160, the road where the burning car was found. Anthony didn't recall what time he'd left his girlfriend's house, but said he drove his gray Dodge 1500 pickup, the car registered to his parents.

Anthony told the detectives that he arrived at the Shell station minutes later. The street, normally congested with traffic and construction trucks, was wide open at this early hour. When he pulled into the station, he said, Craig was already there with Kelly, waiting for him, their Jaguar parked on the south side of the station's mini-mart.

The detectives knew Anthony was painting an incorrect picture. Police had been tipped that he had rendezvoused with Craig and Kelly at that gas station. Authorities didn't disclose where they'd gotten the information, but it was good enough to prompt them to request the store's video surveillance tapes for the early morning hours of Wednesday, December 14.

The tapes clearly showed that Craig and Kelly were not there waiting for Anthony as he was now claiming. Rather, they indicated that at 4:12 a.m., a gray Dodge pickup—matching Anthony's truck—had pulled into the parking lot first, followed by a red four-door that looked very much like a Jaguar. The truck pulled up to the west side of the lot, while the red car drove out of the camera's view toward the south side.

Confronted with the discrepancy, Anthony changed his account to say that Craig and Kelly had followed him to the Shell station. Once there, Anthony said, he'd filled a small red gas can that he kept in his truck. Craig had not asked Anthony to bring a gas can; he knew that Anthony carried one.

(Police later found another security tape raising additional questions about Anthony's account. Looking at tapes from the Green Valley Grocery, detectives found no sign of Melissa or Kelly around the time that Kelly said she had dropped her off. But the next morning, Anthony appears on the tape, wearing a black leather jacket, blue plaid pajama bottoms and athletic shoes, buying something at the register at 3:41 a.m.—just minutes after Kelly had purchased the lighter fluid across the street.)

In any event, at the Shell station a few minutes after the Green Valley stop, Anthony placed the gas can in the center console of his truck and got in, while Craig and Kelly walked toward their Jaguar, Anthony told the detectives. Anthony received a call in seconds from Craig telling him to turn right onto Blue Diamond Highway and head for the mountains toward Pahrump.

For approximately the next twenty-five minutes, Anthony drove with the gasoline at his side, going over the mountains and down to the desert, the lights of Pahrump off to the north. As the road began to flatten out, Anthony got another call from Craig telling him to get off the road. In the rearview mirror, Anthony saw the Jaguar.

Anthony turned his truck onto a dirt road, drove a ways, then stopped. The Jaguar pulled up behind him. Kelly got out and climbed into the front seat of the truck. She told Anthony to turn around, which he did, so that the truck now faced the Jaguar on the dirt road.

Anthony started to say something to Kelly when Craig suddenly came up to the window and asked for the gas can. Anthony passed it to him through the window. Kelly told Anthony to pull forward, about two car lengths away from the Jaguar. As he did this, Anthony asked Kelly what was going on. She wouldn't tell him, according to Anthony.

A few moments later, Craig ran up to Anthony's side of the truck, hopped into the passenger seat by climbing over Anthony, and planted himself ncxt to Kelly.

"Go, go, go!" Craig shouted.

Anthony left the scene, going over the bumpy road back to State Route 160, and headed toward Las Vegas. He could see a glow behind him.

That was the first time, he told the detectives, he realized what might have happened.

They went over the mountains, and when they got to Craig and Kelly's house, Anthony dropped them off. They invited him in, but he declined.

After that, he went home and crawled back into bed.

He claimed he knew nothing about a body being in the trunk until later.

O'Kelley asked Anthony if he would allow police to photograph his truck. He said that was OK, but cautioned it was not in the same condition as the morning of the fire. He said he had changed all four tires because he'd had a blowout the day after the fire. He said two of the tires had been left at a Discount Tire store and the other two at a friend's house.

With that, the interview was over. The detectives left. Anthony Gross was not arrested—yet.

POLICE CONDUCTED ONE MORE INTERVIEW THAT Monday. Meeting at the homicide office, Greg Ruiz, Craig's friend and partner in the Ice Gear clothing store, said he had been contacted by Craig that previous Saturday morning. According to a police affidavit's account of the interview, they'd arranged to meet at a Subway sandwich shop, where Craig and Kelly were waiting when Greg arrived.

Greg drove the couple back to his house. Craig explained that he had traded in his Dodge truck for a new vehicle and was planning to leave the country, but would first drive to Boston to meet a friend, whom police later identified as Craig's former party promoter partner Matt Cline. Craig told Ruiz that the friend would help him liquidate his assets and get him to a country that didn't have an extradition policy with the United States, according to the affidavit.

When they arrived at the house, Ruiz told police Craig said something else: "I'm guilty."

THE INTERVIEWS WITH MANDY POLK, ANTHONY Gross and Gregory Ruiz more than filled in the gaps. They painted Craig and Kelly as directly responsible for setting fire to the Jaguar with Melissa James' body in the trunk, then lying to police, none too convincingly, to avoid bad publicity and to protect Kelly's fading fitness career. Detectives now had plenty of material with which to confront the couple, perhaps enough to arrest them—though probably not for murder.

Neither Mandy nor Anthony, nor any of the phone records, nor anything that Craig and Kelly had said, proved that the couple had *killed* Melissa—they only provided information suggesting the couple had disposed of the body of a woman who'd already died of a drug overdose in their home.

Even if they wanted to go after lesser charges, police had no physical evidence to corroborate the statements of Mandy and Anthony. While Mandy appeared credible enough, Anthony had, police said, fudged some of his statements, and the many calls between him and Craig in the twenty-four hours before Melissa's death raised questions of whether Anthony was truthful despite his cooperation with police.

Then there was the question of motive. Craig had admitted to having an affair with Melissa, and both Craig and Kelly had complained that she was stealing from them. In the context of two successful, high-profile semi-celebrities, the affair/theft motive appeared wobbly. Did something else happen in the hours before Melissa was killed that these witnesses didn't know about—or weren't disclosing?

The problem was time. Both Mandy Polk and Gregory Ruiz had told police that Craig and Kelly weren't going to wait around to find out what police came up with. They planned to flee, for either a non-extradition country, according to Mandy, or to Massachusetts to hook up with Craig's old friend Matt Cline.

Police would need more evidence, and they needed it fast.

Reviewing what they had gleaned from their interviews, a lead came from something Mandy Polk had said. She recounted that Kelly was concerned—"fucked" was how she'd put it—because Kelly had purchased lighter fluid with her credit card at Wal-Mart. Police checked the phone book.

There was a Wal-Mart a quarter-mile away from Craig and Kelly's home.

And it was open twenty-four hours.

CHAPTER SEVENTEEN

ON TUESDAY, DECEMBER 20, 2005, ONE WEEK AFTER Melissa James had telephoned her mother for the last time, police spoke to Robin Peterson, asset protection associate for the Wal-Mart that anchored a sprawling new shopping center at 5200 South Fort Apache Road, just around the corner from the couple's house.

Police had one question: Would the store have any record of somebody buying lighter fluid early the morning of Wednesday, December 14, 2004?

It turned out that the Wal-Mart had as many eyes-in-the-sky as a casino floor. A collection of thirty-one Pan/Tilt/Zoom cameras, or PTZs, scanned the inside at all times. Many more stationary cameras recorded activities at fixed locations. Outside, two additional PTZs and nine stationary cameras kept watch over the parking lot.

Peterson told police—and later explained to a grand jury—that each camera recorded for twenty-four hours on VHS tape, with the time stamped on the tape. On the last day of every month, security officials checked the clocks—they are sometimes four minutes fast or slow—and reset them.

So on the mid-month morning of Wednesday, December 14, the clocks on the Wal-Mart cameras could only have been a minute or two off, at the most.

Even more accurate were the cash registers' internal clocks, hooked electronically to the main corporate clock.

If somebody bought something with a credit card, Wal-Mart would not only know when it had happened to the second, it would probably also have video of it.

When presented by Sergeant Rocky Alby with Kelly Ryan's Visa card number and the approximate time that she would have been in the store, Peterson scoured the electronic journal of sales records on Wal-Mart's computer system and reviewed the security tapes.

At 3:21 a.m., a security camera picked up a woman with dark shoulder-length hair, wearing a red sweatsuit with a white stripe down the side, pushing a cart full of white bottles through the seasonal Lawn & Garden section at the southern end of the store, next to the nursery.

Ten minutes later, at 3:31 a.m., the cashier rang up a purchase of goods from that same department charged to Kelly Ryan's Visa: six 64-ounce bottles of Kingsford Charcoal Lighter Fluid, one 64-ounce bottle of Premium Quality charcoal lighter fluid, a barbecue tool set and a bottle of juice.

A security camera in the parking lot then picked up the same woman—the time on the tape, 3:31 a.m., is off by about a minute—pushing the cart to a red mid-sized car that looked very much like an X-Type Jaguar. Another camera showed a burly man in a dark shirt, light jacket and dark baseball cap meeting the woman at the car and helping her put the items in the back seat.

The woman got into the passenger seat, the man in the driver's seat, and the car drove out of the Wal-Mart parking lot at 3:36 a.m.

Within the hour, a trucker would report a Jaguar ablaze on Sandy Valley Road.

Looking at the tapes closely, detectives were almost certain the woman was Kelly Ryan, the man Craig Titus.

It may not be all the evidence police would need for a murder conviction. But it was enough for arrests.

Anthony Gross, who had been cooperating with police, was arrested without incident and booked into the Clark County Detention Center on charges of accessory to murder and third-degree arson in the death of Melissa James. He was not charged with murder.

Police also went to arrest Craig Titus and Kelly Ryan.

Through interviews, police found that the couple had spent the Wednesday night they had been interviewed with a friend named Jeffrey Schwimmer, a cousin of *Friends* star David Schwimmer.

They spent Thursday night at the house being rented to Mandy and Ryan, and Friday night at the Holiday Inn, where Ryan had paid cash.

After that, they were gone.

CHAPTER EIGHTEEN

CRAIG TITUS HAD NEVER CALLED RON AVIDAN BACK, which was unusual. Craig was not one to pass up free publicity. He had phoned Ron at his office the evening of Monday, December 12, to talk about his new women's fitness organization. Ron had asked to him to call back later when he could record the interview for the Getbig.com website.

After a week, Ron had still not heard from Craig.

Then, on the morning of Monday, December 19, 2005, Ron got an email from a contact in the body-building industry asking if hc had heard anything about Craig Titus getting into trouble with the law. Ron asked what kind of trouble. The contact said he had heard it had something to do with murder.

Ron dismissed it. Like so many in the industry, Ron Avidan knew about Craig's reputation, his temper, his feuds with everybody from Lonnie Teper to Ron Harris to King Kamali. He knew about Craig's criminal past. He had heard the reports about Craig punching people and the rumors about his sexual escapades. He had heard the scuttlebutt about Craig using drugs.

But murder? Ridiculous.

The running joke in the bodybuilding industry is that every day, according to the message boards, somebody is said to be getting arrested, divorced or killed, only for it to be revealed later that the reports were untrue. Ron Avidan tried to edit out the more outrageous of the postings, and delete the ones that turned out to be bogus, but rumors still flourished.

Craig Titus being involved in murder seemed like one more crazy report, perhaps generated by one of Craig's detractors.

Then throughout that Monday more reports came in to Getbig.com. Craig wasn't returning people's phone calls, and neither was Kelly.

Ron himself tried to call him, but got only voice mail. His emails to Craig weren't returned.

Soon, it was looking like some of these reports to Getbig.com were more than just far-fetched rumors. A number of bodybuilders had made Las Vegas home, and many of them knew and socialized with cops, themselves often gym rats. Now bloggers were saying they had heard reports from within the department that police were investigating the fire of a 2003 Jaguar out in the desert nearly a week earlier.

Kelly Ryan was famous for her 2003 red Jaguar—Dan Solomon had mentioned it in his story about Craig and Kelly just a year earlier.

One blogger had heard there was a body in the trunk and that the car had been stolen. Others started hearing that police were talking to Craig's friends.

By Tuesday, December 20, people in the bodybuilding industry were asking their police sources about the reports—and the police weren't denying them.

And all the while, Craig and Kelly weren't answering their phones or emails. Their silence fueled speculation. Some thought Craig and Kelly were in jail, others that one or both of them had died.

Finally, on Wednesday, December 21, 2005, Las Vegas police sent out this press release:

LAS VEGAS METROPOLITAN POLICE DEPARTMENT

MEDIA RELEASE

DECEMBER 21, 2005

EVENT #: 051214-0619
FOR IMMEDIATE RELEASE
Lt. Tom Monahan
Homicide Section . . .

On December 14, 2005 at approximately 4:40 a.m., a trucker was traveling on State Route 160 (Blue Diamond Rd) from Pahrump toward Las Vegas, when he spotted a fire in the desert about a half-mile from the road. When firefighters extinguished the blaze, they observed what appeared to be human remains in the trunk of the car.

The remains were confirmed to be that of a human, and under the circumstances, it is being investigated as a homicide. . . .

Investigation into above incident has resulted in arrest warrants being issued for three suspects.

1. *Titus, Craig Michael, DOB: 01/14/1965, 5ft 8 inches, 225 lbs., brown hair with hazel eyes. Hair is very short.*

2. *Ryan, Kelly Ann, DOB: 07/10/1972, 5ft 3 inches, 120 lbs., brown hair with green eyes.*

Titus has a no-bail arrest warrant charging him with murder and third degree arson.

Ryan has a no-bail arrest warrant charging her with accessory to murder and third degree arson.

A third suspect has been identified as 23 year old Anthony Gross. Gross is in custody and has been booked into the Clark County Detention Center on charges of accessory to murder and third degree arson.

Craig Titus and Kelly Ryan are husband and wife and were living in the southwest area of Las Vegas. Both are successful body builders and hold numerous titles in the body building and fitness industry.

At this time it is unclear where the two suspects may have fled.

To people in the bodybuilding community the press release seemed unreal: Murder? Arson? Accessory? Fled?

Even to Craig's biggest critics, the words seemed incredible.

That Kelly Ryan could be involved was inconceivable.

Suddenly there were more questions than answers.

According to the press release, the murder had occurred just two days after Craig had spoken to Ron Avidan, who didn't sense anything was wrong.

What happened? Had Craig snapped?

And who was killed? The press release didn't name a victim. Early speculation was that it could have been Craig's daughter, Ashley. But soon her well-being was confirmed. So who had been in that trunk?

And who was Anthony Gross? His name meant nothing in the bodybuilding industry. None of Craig and Kelly's friends in bodybuilding had ever heard them talk about him.

Bodybuilding had been rocked before by steroid scandals and petty feuds, but nothing like this.

"I was looking at Getbig.com," recalls Lonnie Teper. "Somebody wrote a post: 'Craig Titus on the run for murder.' And you always look at these things and go, 'Come on.' Most of the people who post on this website are morons. They can't wait to trash you or write bad things. They have no life other than sitting on there all day long. I look at this thing: Yeah, right. There was always somebody dying who wasn't dying.

"Then," says Teper, "I started getting calls: 'Did you hear about Craig and Kelly?' I called Jay Cutler, who lived in Las Vegas. I said, 'Is this true?' He said, 'Yeah.'

"The more I was looking at it, the more I thought this was a fairy tale. This was a fantasy land thing. This doesn't make any sense at all, these things I'm reading. I know he had a bad temper; he wanted to punch me out a couple of times, but I didn't think he was capable of murder."

Shawn Ray says that he also heard about it on the

Internet. He was logged on to the MuscleMayhem site, which was reporting rumors that Craig Titus was in trouble with police.

"Muscle Mayhem transferred it over to Getbig.com, and it mushroomed from there," says Shawn. "We have two friends on the police force in Las Vegas, and they confirmed that their car was found and it was Kelly's. That's how I confirmed it. When I knew it was Kelly's, I knew Craig and Kelly couldn't be far behind, because the car was never reported stolen. I took that rumor and went straight to some credible sources on the police force, and Craig and Kelly hadn't been arrested at that time, but the car was confirmed."

Shawn called around to friends in bodybuilding to share information.

"Nobody I talked to was surprised that Craig would be involved," he says. "A lot of people were surprised that Kelly would be involved."

Ron Harris says he was logged on to either Getbig or MuscleMania when he saw the press release about Craig being wanted for murder.

"I didn't even give him the benefit of the doubt," Ron said. "If I had ever seen just the headline, 'Pro Bodybuilder Charged with Murder,' I have to say he's probably the first guy I would have thought of. His temper— It's just he's always seemed like a very hostile, angry guy, and I always thought it was a good thing he was in bodybuilding, because he had a good way to channel that in training, but I guess it wasn't good enough."

But the fact that Kelly was also wanted in a murder was a "huge shock."

"I knew her way back when she was that sweet little girl from North Carolina," he says.

Dan Solomon says he got a phone call from his radio co-host Bob Cicherillo "telling me he got an email that he was about to inform me of the most impossible, the most horrible, the most tragic story that I could ever even fathom."

It was one of the early reports of a car on fire and Craig being involved. Dan refused to believe it. The couple had been on his radio show just three months earlier talking up big plans about a new fitness organization.

"When I challenged Bob, he told me that a body was found in the trunk of Kelly's Jaguar," says Dan. "And at first, I doubted it, because this industry is just, you know, loaded with all sorts of rumor mills and speculation. And every week, somebody is rumored to be dead or something like that. So you kind of take it with a grain of salt."

Dan text-messaged Kelly, and "I didn't get a response back," he says. "And I put in the call and didn't get a response back. And I was desperately trying to find out if this was fact or fiction. And obviously, it was only another day or so that passed before the story [appeared] in the various newspapers."

With so many unanswered questions, the bodybuilding industry rumor mill went into overdrive. According to Ron Avidan, the Internet boards gushed wild speculation. He tried to bring some reason to the situation, writing on his website:

In Craig and Kelly's defense, none of these rumors are facts. We don't know how or in what way they were involved, and in my book, they are innocent until proven guilty. Speaking for myself, Craig & Kelly have always been warm and friendly to me, and I can't think of them getting involved in this unless it was accidental. What happened—I don't know, but hopefully soon, the truth will come out.

Ron called on the couple to "come forward and face the charges" as the bodybuilding community reeled.

In speaking with a lot of people today, although there are many people who think Craig is capable of these allegations, there are just as many people and fans that want Craig to know that they are supporting him and Kelly, and do care about them. Many of them are just horrified and stunned on the turn of events.

Obviously, more to come on this sad event.

THE NEXT DAY, WEDNESDAY, THE NEWS WOULD LEAP from the bodybuilding websites to the mainstream press, with the first story on the case in the *Las Vegas Review-Journal*.

Headlined "Muscular suspects sought in slaying," the story aimed straight at the notoriety of the couple:

Las Vegans Craig Titus and Kelly Ryan, bodybuilding champions who have graced the covers of numerous national magazines, gained new titles on Wednesday: murder suspects.

Las Vegas police were hunting for the high-profile couple Wednesday in connection with a body found last week in the trunk of a torched 2003 Jaguar. The 5-foot-8 inch, 250-pound Titus and his chiseled 120-pound wife are both charged in arrest warrants with murder and third-degree arson, according to police.

The story said authorities "have not offered a motive," and were awaiting DNA results before identifying the victim—though it was believed she was a 28-year-old woman who'd lived with the couple. The story noted that Craig was known as "the bad boy of bodybuilding" because of his temper, opinionated nature and "stint in jail."

It was the first of many reports that would irritate those in the know, with Kelly incorrectly identified as a bodybuilding champ rather than the fitness star she really was. It was also the first story, to the chagrin of those in the industry, to raise the specter of steroids.

The *Review-Journal* quoted Craig from an old Body building.com interview as saying: "Point is, every sport has athletes who use performance-enhancing drugs," and noted that the *San Jose Mercury News* had reported that Titus was one of several pro bodybuilders subpoenaed last year in a federal steroids probe.

First the steroid scandal, now this.

The industry was bracing for another black eye.

The situation grew worse the next day, Friday, December 23, with news reports about Craig and Kelly's statements to police contained in the just-released "Declaration of Warrants/Summons" written by Detective Dean O'Kelley.

The declaration laid out virtually the entire case against Craig and Kelly, including grim details of the fire, with O'Kelley describing the discovery of the "burned remains of an unidentified person" who was "most likely female" in the trunk area.

Identifying the presumed victim for the first time, the declaration recounted the detectives' interviews with Craig and Kelly—how they both "believed their live-in personal assistant, Melissa James, had taken the car from the garage without [their] permission."

O'Kelley documented the couple's assertions that Melissa had been stealing from them, but pointedly added, "No report of the embezzlement was made to the police." Nor did they report the allegedly stolen Jaguar.

Most potentially damaging for Craig was the detective's characterization of the bodybuilder's relationship with Melissa.

"Titus admitted to Detective C. Mogg he was having an affair with James that his wife Ryan did not know about," the declaration said. "He said there has been tension between Ryan and James because of James embezzling money so he had rented a room for James at a La Quinta hotel on West Sahara. He said he had rented the room for two nights and he had spent most of one night [with] James at her room."

The name Melissa James, however, meant nothing to those in the bodybuilding community, who assumed she was little more than another one of Craig's conquests.

"She was nobody from nowhere," said Shawn Ray,

who had no recollection of ever meeting Melissa, "but Craig did say that he had a girl that was going to help him with his Ice Gear clothing store."

"She has lived in Vegas a few times," Matt Cline, one of the few to actually know Melissa, later told Get big.com, portraying her as a methamphetamine addict. "Melissa has been in and out of Craig's life for over ten years. Melissa used to stay in the background, she wasn't one of those people that you would know was around. She was decent looking, but wasn't striking."

Against these harsh portrayals, it would be left to Melissa's mother to provide a softer image.

"You know what's so hard?" she said in a heart-breaking interview with the *Las Vegas Review-Journal* in the days after the news broke. "They burned my daughter so that we can't even see her again before we bury her. She is so sweet. She is so sweet and beautiful. I can't imagine anybody doing that to her."

Detective O'Kelley's declaration made graphically clear that Melissa was more than just burned. It noted that when the body was inspected, "It was discovered the victim's head was encircled with grey duct tape from just above the eyebrows to just below the lower lip of the mouth. A white fabric ligature was tied around the neck of the victim with a partial knot positioned on the left side of the neck."

Ron Avidan, who had spoken to Craig less than two days before the body was found, summed up his reaction this way: "Complete and utter disbelief.

"I had just talked to him. There was no indication anything would happen," he says. "We talked a lot. Everything was fine. Craig was confrontational. But could he kill anybody? No. Was he threatening people? Yeah. He maybe hit somebody. There's a big difference between hitting somebody and strangling somebody. It doesn't make sense. His state of mind that Monday night was definitely not that of somebody who was going to kill someone."

CHAPTER NINETEEN

HAVING GONE PUBLIC, POLICE NOW WERE HOPING that Craig and Kelly would make a mistake and turn up somewhere, tipping their location by using a credit card or making a long-distance phone call. Authorities were still operating under the theory that they were headed to the Boston area, and so the FBI was notified.

Las Vegas detectives developed one lead: Craig had changed wheels. David Levinson, a sales associate at Integrity Chrysler Jeep Dodge, told police he was working on Saturday, December 17, when at about 10 a.m. he had a customer.

It was Craig Titus, whom the salesman knew. Back in April or May, Levinson had sold Craig his 2005 Dodge SRT10 quad cab, a hot-rod truck with a Viper V10 motor, spoiler on the back of the bed and wide tires.

Craig told Levinson he wanted a replacement for the SRT10. He appeared "fatigued, a little skittish, a little jittery," Levinson would later tell a grand jury.

"He expressed that he was under some contact with Metro about somebody that was his roommate, that he was questioned, he wanted to get out of town for a little while and relax," Levinson said. "He stated he was going to get this vehicle and take it to Utah."

Craig explained that his roommate had "probably incurred some violence" or something involving methamphetamine dealing with somebody else. He never gave the roommate's name, but said it was a woman, according to Levinson.

He also said there was a Jaguar that was missing.

"He was looking for something that could go through some rough terrain," Levinson recalled. "As he expressed it, he might be going through some gravel and some rough terrain."

They settled on a 2006 Dodge Mega Cab pickup 2500. By about noon, they started the paperwork for Craig to lease the truck. Craig placed the down payment on his business account, Emperor Enterprises.

Levinson recalled that Craig nodded off, napping at times, while he handled the paperwork.

At 2 p.m., Craig drove off the lot in his new truck.

For the better part of a week, authorities had lost track of Craig and Kelly. The last witness to have seen Craig was Gregory Ruiz, and that was on the day that Craig turned in his truck. In going public, police counted on somebody else having seen or spoken to Craig.

In Boston, FBI agents keeping an eye on Matt Cline's neighborhood caught a break. They spotted Craig's Dodge Mega Cab about a mile away from Cline's house, then lost it.

On Friday morning, the same day that the Las Vegas papers were revealing Craig's admission of an affair with Melissa James, the FBI alerted Las Vegas police with the sighting. Detective Dean O'Kelley, who took the call, was told to stand by and be prepared to fly East.

CRAIG HAD IN FACT BEEN HEADED FOR MATT Cline's house. Around 8 a.m. on that Friday, Matt got a call from Craig saying that he was broke and needed money.

As Matt later told Getbig.com, federal agents had already spoken to Matt. He told Craig that the neighborhood was crawling with agents and it was "not smart" to be around.

"Dude, I just need some money . . . and I will go on my way," Craig said, according to Matt.

Matt told him again: The police knew he was there, the papers knew he and Kelly were headed to Boston, and this was not a place to be. But Craig either didn't want to hear what Matt was saying, or didn't believe him.

"I just talked to my attorney," he told Matt. "They [the police] don't know anything."

"Bullshit," Matt said.

Not long after this conversation, FBI agents arrived at Matt's house, asking him to help catch Craig. Matt told them no way.

CRAIG AND KELLY DIDN'T VENTURE FAR. LATER that morning, they drove to a Jiffy Lube oil-change store in Canton, Massachusetts. They brought their truck into a bay right next to a Massachusetts state trooper who was getting his cruiser's oil changed—and who apparently had no idea that the subjects of a nationwide manhunt were just feet away.

According to Jiffy Lube's manager, Scott Rabb, who later filed an affidavit on behalf of the couple, they didn't act like fugitives from justice.

"Both Mr. Titus and Mrs. Ryan were very relaxed, outgoing and not in a hurry as they talked to myself and my employees," wrote Rabb. "Mrs. Ryan discussed dancing choreography with me as I used to teach a local group, and she demonstrated some of her dance moves in the parking lot facing the main road."

Craig told Rabb that if he were ever in Las Vegas to give him a call; Craig gave him his telephone number, according to Rabb.

"A short time after they left, they returned and Mr. Titus gave me money for a lint roller he took and forgot to pay for," wrote Rabb. "I thanked him for his honesty and was extremely surprised they were the same individuals that were arrested as a result of a warrant from Las Vegas."

At 3:45 p.m., Craig and Kelly had made their way from the Jiffy Lube to a shopping center anchored by Shaw's Supermarket in Stoughton, Massachusetts, fifteen miles south of Boston on Route 138.

Kelly went into a Touch Nails, a salon fronted by a large window, and walked across the black-and-white checkerboard floor to the back of the store to get a pedicure. Craig remained in the truck in the parking lot, drinking a Mug Root Beer. According to the store employees, Kelly asked for a cherry red manicure.

Kelly Ryan was just taking her seat when the SWAT

team arrived. The agents stormed the nail salon, startling the store's employees and scaring the customers so badly that owner William Ho later complained to *The Boston Globe* that "most of my customers are not coming back."

Kelly was arrested without a struggle.

Craig was arrested in the parking lot without incident.

The couple were brought in to the Canton Police Department while the truck was searched by the FBI. In it, agents found Craig's passport and 83 one-hundred-dollar bills hidden in a false bottom of an aerosol can.

They posed for booking photographs. Craig appeared as he always did, confident, tough, his head shaved, his face showing stubble. Kelly looked dazed, her eyebrows pencil-thin, her puffy-lipped mouth flat, expressionless.

AFTERWARDS, MATT CLINE SAID HE FELT TERRIBLE.

"This whole thing is a fucking nightmare," he told Getbig.com. "The FBI basically followed the bread crumbs from Las Vegas to Boston in order to get Craig and Kelly."

But he wanted to make one thing clear: "I did not rat out Craig and Kelly. I did not want anything to do with this at all, and in no way was I part of that. Craig has been my friend for over sixteen years, and I don't like to hear rumors that I ratted out my friend. It just did not happen."

For Ron Harris, the arrest hit close to home—literally. The man with whom he had sparred off-and-on for a decade was pinched not far from Harris' house. Harris recalled that somebody called him to say that his "friend" was on television—local television.

"I go: 'What are you talking about?' " Harris recalls. "Because everybody was speculating about where they were. A lot of people thought they were in Mexico by then, because with Nevada, Las Vegas and Mexico is a few hours' drive, it's nothing major. Or maybe they had already gotten to Europe or something like that. I never would have thought they would have gone friggin' cross-country all the way up here in my backyard practically, of all places."

Harris' wife used to get her nails done at the salon where Kelly was arrested. Ron got his hair cut at the Supercuts in that shopping center were Craig was arrested in the parking lot.

"I drive past that place where they were apprehended about five times a day on average," says Harris.

When Shawn Ray heard about the couple's arrest, he was struck by what might have been. He suddenly realized that he had signed up Craig and Kelly for the bodybuilding camp in Dubai, but had to cancel it when one of the other organizers injured his back.

Kelly's former coach Keith Kephart was just getting off the golf course when his friend Ken Taylor, who'd promoted Kelly's first fitness show—recruiting her personally to participate—called and left a voice mail message saying that the couple had been arrested.

"I was just utterly stunned," says Keith. "And so then I hurried home. And of course, by the time I got home, I had about five emails from people with the same information."

As stunned as Craig and Kelly's colleagues in body-building were at the arrest, an even greater surprise awaited them.

The couple would again talk to the police, without lawyers.

This time, what they had to say would send shockwaves across the industry.

CHAPTER TWENTY

THE FBI WASTED NO TIME. NOT LONG AFTER CRAIG and Kelly were hauled into the Canton Police Department station, agents sat them down for interviews, not waiting for Las Vegas detectives to arrive.

That night, Detectives Dean O'Kelley and Cliff Mogg flew from Las Vegas to Boston in the hopes of speaking to Craig and Kelly themselves. On the plane, they read the FBI report of the questioning earlier in the day.

The FBI, which apparently didn't tape-record the interviews—not uncommon practice by the agency—portrayed Craig as cocky and profane.

When he was asked why he and Kelly fled, Craig said, "I wasn't going back to jail for no fucking body."

Kelly appeared more restrained. She told the agent that while on the road, Craig had slept in the truck, avoiding motels because "they were afraid of being recognized," according to the FBI report. Kelly told the agent they'd planned to return West to pick up her dog, then they were headed to Mexico.

Other statements seemed ambiguous at best, with Craig agreeing to leading questions by the FBI agent, who suggested to Craig that Melissa may have died during kinky sex.

"You were having kinky sex together and something went wrong?" the agent said, according to excerpts printed in the *Las Vegas Review-Journal*. "You were having sex. You had her tied up. You were using drugs and maybe she OD'd?" the agent asked.

The agent's report said, "Titus responded words to the effect, 'Yeah, we were having sex and she OD'd. Let's go with that. That's a good story.' After making this statement, Titus paused for a moment and then stated, 'No more questions.' "

The next day, Saturday—Christmas Eve day—Craig and Kelly agreed to talk to the hometown detectives. Again, no lawyer was present, even though Craig had paid a $5,000 retainer for a Las Vegas attorney.

This interview, like the first ones they'd given the day the body was found, was tape-recorded. According to a detailed account of the interviews by the *Review-Journal*, Craig came off as arrogant and unrepentant—and fully admitted what Mandy Polk had told detectives earlier: that Craig and Kelly had disposed of the body of Melissa James.

According to the *Review-Journal*, Craig told the detectives that he had Melissa "in the fucking car, dead, stinking up my fucking car," the needle still sticking in her arm.

Panicked and feeling "fucking ruined"—not to

mention angry that "my car's ruined"—Craig decided to put her in the trunk, set fire to the car and "play stupid."

He admitted the process was "fucking gross." He put her in the fetal position, wrapped her up in a blanket, tape, wire and his bathrobe belt, and shoved her in the Jaguar trunk, all while Kelly cried hysterically.

Asked why he did it, Craig insisted he'd had no choice; he had to spare Kelly from bad publicity.

"She is the number-one fitness athlete in the world," Craig said, according to the *Review-Journal*. "Highly respected in the sport, and if you think of fitness, Kelly Ryan. Period. . . . And here we walk in our garage and our friend's OD'd in our fucking car. So if that gets out to the public, we're ruined."

He admitted that it all looked horrible, but insisted that neither he nor Kelly had murdered Melissa, that all they did was dispose of the body of a woman whose abuse of crystal methamphetamines, OxyContin, Nubain, cocaine and morphine finally caught up to her—in their own house.

"If I really wanted to . . . burn her, and it was a murder, I would've dug a hole out in the desert and dumped her in the hole, and burned my car myself," Titus said, according to the *Review-Journal*. "It doesn't take a fucking genius to know— Well, you know, if you're gonna murder somebody, you don't put her in your car and burn her."

"Unless somebody panics," a detective said.

"Yeah, well, unless they're really stupid."

In her interview, Kelly covered much of the same ground, also admitting that they'd found Melissa dead from an overdose, and saying they'd not only worried about the publicity from her death, but also feared police would find Melissa's drugs—and Craig's steroids—if they searched the house, and possibly send him back to prison.

Kelly painted a horrifying picture of the body's disposal, talking about how Melissa wasn't even stiff when Craig bound her. But she made it clear that the decision, though made in panic, was mutual, and admitted to buying the lighter fluid at Wal-Mart.

The only time Kelly stopped answering questions was when Detective O'Kelley tried to get her to turn on her husband.

"You can't be held responsible for what another person does unless you choose to," O'Kelley told her, according to the *Review-Journal*. "And, this is your opportunity to back up, as far as you can, and make it right."

"I don't want to give a statement without anyone here . . . my lawyer," she said.

THREE DAYS LATER, ON TUESDAY, DECEMBER 27, Craig and Kelly finally had lawyers. The attorneys were hired for the couple's first court appearance since being arrested, an arraignment in district court in Stoughton, Massachusetts. It was also the first time most people had seen the couple since the after-party at the Olympia more than a year earlier.

This couple who once symbolized the ultimate picture of all that was manhood and womanhood looked tired, haggard, small, old.

As supporters in the courtroom wept, the judge read

the charges against Craig and Kelly, and denied them bail.

Afterwards, Craig's lawyer, Bobby A. George, launched damage control, saying that Craig denied any romantic involvement with Melissa around the time of her death—despite what Craig had said to police the day her body was found—and suggested that the couple had never fled from police.

George, one of the Boston area's most prominent criminal defense lawyers, said the $8,300 in the car couldn't get anyone far, much less overseas. He said once the couple had found out about the fugitive warrant, they were ready to go back to Las Vegas and talk to police—but police got to them first.

Asked why they went East in the first place, George told reporters, "They were here to see friends during the holiday."

Kelly's lawyer, John Gibbons, added that "she had no idea" about the arrest warrant.

A CONTINENT AWAY, ANOTHER HEARING WAS HELD, this one for Anthony Gross. it was about the same case, but the outcome was much different.

While Craig and Kelly remained locked in a Massachusetts jail, Anthony, to the great relief of his family, was ordered to house arrest by Justice of the Peace Joseph Bonaventure on $13,000 bail.

From her home in New Jersey, Melissa's mother, Maura James, watched the case unfold with a mixture of sadness, revulsion and anger.

"Whoever did this," she told the Associated Press, "I want them to pay."

◆ ◆ ◆

IT WAS NOT GOING TO BE THAT EASY. IN BUILDING A case against Craig, Kelly and Anthony, police had plenty of evidence to arrest them, on the basis of the statements by Anthony Gross himself, Mandy Polk and Gregory Ruiz, as well as the phone records and the fact that Craig and Kelly had fled. Prosecutors also felt they had sufficient evidence to hold the couple on murder and other charges, based on the admissions to the Las Vegas detectives during their post-arrest questioning. Anthony Gross' admissions, combined with the reduced charges, suggested a plea deal was in the works for him.

But while the police were satisfied they had probable cause for arrest, and courts found enough evidence to hold Craig and Kelly without bail, there remained scant evidence that a murder had been committed, by Craig and Kelly, or anybody else for that matter.

The autopsy was inconclusive. The coroner couldn't tell what had killed Melissa James: strangulation or drug overdose or something else. There was no eyewitness to the murder, no murder weapon, not even any evidence of murder, or even assault, in the couple's house.

Should the case go to trial at that moment, prosecutors could build a convincing argument that Craig and Kelly had shown suspicious behavior and horribly bad judgment, but that might be all. The act was horrific, the lies suspicious, but it was a far cry from first-degree murder. The more compelling explanation may be the one to which the couple had admitted: that in a panic, they'd disposed of an already dead body.

As before, when police were working toward arresting the couple, detectives needed more evidence if they wanted the murder charges to stick.

With the case now garnering widespread publicity, from local television stations in Boston and Las Vegas, to the *Los Angeles Times* and *People* magazine, something, somewhere, was bound to materialize for police.

They would find it in a gym bag.

CHAPTER TWENTY-ONE

ON THE DAY THAT THE PRESS RELEASE CAME OUT announcing that police were searching for Craig Titus and Kelly Ryan in the murder of a woman, one of Kelly's closest friends picked up the phone and called a lawyer.

That lawyer then called homicide detectives.

Megan Pierson did not want to believe that Kelly Ryan, who was to be matron of honor at her wedding in less than two months, was capable of murder. And so when she initially spoke to detectives she didn't tell them everything she knew.

But the more she thought about it, the more she told. Her words would fill in the final gaps in the investigation.

In an account that she later repeated for a grand jury, Megan began by explaining to police that she'd idolized Kelly Ryan. As a figure competitor, Megan had looked at Flyin' Ryan as a role model and an inspiration. After meeting her in that Mexican restaurant, Kelly had become a coach, workout partner and dear friend.

Speaking to Detective Dean O'Kelley, Megan said that on Monday, December 12, 2005, at around 5 p.m., she'd trained with Kelly in the couple's fancy home gym as they had done many times before. Craig may have been there. This was around the time that he was on the phone with Ron Avidan of Getbig.com, calling the bodybuilding blogger at work to discuss the new women's fitness organization, with Ron asking Craig to call him back later.

As Megan and Kelly trained, Megan picked up on a strange vibe. Kelly started talking, seemingly out of the blue, about Melissa James, who Megan knew lived there. Megan had seen her a couple of times when coming over to work out, but knew little about her.

Now, Kelly was complaining that Melissa had made strange purchases on Kelly's credit cards. Kelly said she had confronted Melissa, who pleaded ignorance. It was the first time that Kelly had ever complained about Melissa, Megan told the detective.

After the workout, Megan left the house. What she didn't know—but police now did—was that later that evening, Craig had brought Melissa to the La Quinta Inn, where she stayed in room 232, the room billed to Craig's company card. Craig had said he left at about 1 or 2 a.m., then came back to the motel at about 10 a.m. on Tuesday to pick up Melissa and bring her back to the house.

According to Megan, around this same time Tuesday morning she'd received a phone call from Craig. She wasn't answering her phone at the time and Craig had left a message to call him. She found this strange. They saw each other when she trained at the house, but she didn't speak to him much and he'd perhaps called her once in the last month.

Megan returned the call, not to Craig, but to Kelly, around 10 a.m. on Tuesday, December 13. Kelly resumed her rant from the evening before about Melissa, saying that they had found suspicious things in her room.

About an hour later, around 11 a.m., Megan called Craig, who elaborated on what these things were. He said Kelly had gone into Melissa's room and found an open lock box with credit cards, bank records and papers for a home equity line of credit. He told her that Florida authorities wanted Melissa for identity theft.

With anger in his voice, Craig snarled that there were three things you didn't mess with: his friends, family and money, according to Megan.

The detective would note that the timing of these conversations conflicted with the account given by Craig and Kelly, who said they hadn't gone through Melissa's room until after Kelly dropped her off at the grocery store around 3:30 p.m.

It was but a small point. Megan would provide bigger ones.

After those phone calls, Megan went to the University of Nevada, Las Vegas to attend a 2 p.m. final exam, one of her last tests before graduation. Either before or after the test, she recalled, she'd phoned Kelly to ask about their usual 5 p.m. workout. Megan had wanted to follow the session with a get-together to celebrate her graduation.

Five o'clock came and went, and Kelly never called back. Always conscientious about returning phone calls, Kelly's inaction struck Megan as odd.

Megan made reservations anyway at a restaurant at

the Green Valley Ranch, a casino hotel just outside Las Vegas. She and her fiancé, Jeremy Foley, were just sitting down for dinner at around 6:30 p.m. when Megan's cell phone rang.

It was Craig, calling from his home phone, according to the caller ID. When Megan answered, Craig started talking, for no apparent reason, about Melissa again. He said that he had bought Melissa a plane ticket to Florida, but then said Melissa had been dropped off at a grocery store nearby. He said the couple didn't feel sorry for her because she'd stolen from them.

He said the couple had found evidence of a $23,000 wire transfer, but didn't know where the money had gone. Megan, a mortgage broker experienced in wire transfers, didn't believe Craig, but urged him, if he was really concerned, to call the police. They ended their conversation.

Megan and her fiancé got only another fifteen minutes of peace when her cell phone rang yet again. This time it was Kelly, "extremely pissed off," Megan would later say. Kelly said that Melissa had threatened to kill her. Kelly handed the phone to Craig, who continued to complain about Melissa.

Megan then heard nothing on the line for a moment. Then, in the background, Megan could hear Craig asking Kelly if Megan and her fiancé could come over to the house after their dinner. He got back on the line and said that Kelly wasn't feeling well and that perhaps they could get together the next night. Then Craig abruptly hung up.

Later, Megan got yet another call at dinner, this time from Kelly, apparently feeling better, yet still weirdly full of anger at Melissa. She stopped complaining about her housemate long enough to invite Megan and Jeremy over after all.

Despite the three odd phone calls at dinner, and other strange conversations earlier in the day with Craig and Kelly, Megan nonetheless decided to join them after dinner. Kelly was her best friend. There must be some reason for these strange outbursts about Melissa James, a woman Megan didn't even know.

After dinner, Megan and her fiancé went home, picked up their puppy, then arrived at Craig and Kelly's house around 10:30 or 11 p.m. Craig was "a little disturbed" when they got there, Megan would recall, still agitated over Melissa.

He showed Megan and Jeremy why he was so upset: a bag of crystal meth and bloody needles that he said belonged to Melissa.

It was the start of a surreal Tuesday evening, reminiscent of the weird Thursday night that Mandy Polk would describe.

Megan told the detective that everybody had gone upstairs, with Jeremy talking to Craig in the office area and Megan going into the master bedroom to speak with Kelly, who was in the bathroom, wearing a dark sweatsuit. Kelly was drying her hair and putting on lotion and makeup as if she had just gotten out of the shower.

Kelly spoke very quietly so that, Megan sensed, Craig couldn't hear her. Occasionally, Craig walked in, and she'd stop talking.

In this hushed voice, and in between Craig's interruptions, Kelly started telling Megan more about Melissa.

Kelly said the couple had gotten a motel room for her the night before, and that Craig had gone to that room to confront Melissa about the drugs and the theft. The next day, Craig had brought Melissa back to the house. Melissa walked upstairs to where Kelly was.

According to Kelly, Melissa was armed with a Taser gun.

Kelly said she'd snatched it away, turned it on and fired it into the back of Melissa's neck. But the gun hadn't been set high enough, so the jolt only got Melissa's attention.

Kelly said she'd yelled for Craig, who bounded upstairs, picked up Melissa, carried her downstairs into the living room, body-slammed her, professional wrestler–style, into the floor and beat her up, according to Megan.

What was so strange, Megan told the detective, was that as Kelly related this incredible story, she calmly folded clothes in her bedroom.

A couple of times Craig came into the room, and Kelly abruptly talked about work or training, then returned to her tale of the Taser and the body-slam. At one point, both Craig and Jeremy came into the room, and Kelly brought Megan into the walk-in closet, closed the doors and whispered the rest of the story.

Kelly told Megan that Melissa had survived the beating and body-slamming by Craig, taken a Xanax and gone to sleep.

Kelly then admitted going into Melissa's room and punching her in the face.

At some point, either before or after the Xanax, another struggle had broken out with Melissa—or maybe it was the same one; Kelly was rambling, according to Megan.

Kelly said that Craig had held down Melissa while telling Kelly to get morphine. Kelly shot an entire syringe of morphine into Melissa's leg, but Melissa was resilient to the drug, Kelly said, and needed a big dose.

Megan told the detective that none of what Kelly was telling her upstairs made any sense. Kelly didn't say why she'd suddenly Tasered Melissa, why Craig had hurt her, why Kelly had gone back for more, or why she'd injected Melissa with morphine.

Kelly just said that that's what had happened that day. As proof, she showed Megan marks on her knuckles from punching Melissa.

Finally, Megan asked Kelly where Melissa was.

"She's downstairs," Kelly whispered.

Megan assumed that meant that Melissa was in her room asleep. The room was next to the door to the garage, and when Megan then walked downstairs with Kelly, she noticed that the door was closed. Megan didn't go inside.

At about this point, Megan told the detective, it was late at night, close to midnight. Craig, she said, had left the house for about ten minutes, driving his truck. When he returned, Megan asked him what he was doing. He only said that what he did was no big deal.

Kelly then brought Megan into the kitchen to show her more of what Kelly felt was evidence of Melissa's evil ways: drinking glasses covered in a film that

Kelly believed was morphine, placed there by Melissa to poison the couple. Kelly said she'd sipped from those glasses and could taste something different, Megan told the detective.

Kelly also told Megan that the couple had found a brochure for a water softener company in Melissa's room, leading them to suspect she was tampering with the household water supply. Kelly brought Megan and her fiancé, Jeremy, into the three-car garage—the doors were closed at this late hour—to check the water softener.

The garage was illuminated by Kelly's posing lights, which she shined on herself to practice the moves that she would use for the judges. The Jaguar was parked there. Jeremy inspected the salt supply in the water softener. He lifted the lid off the bin with the salt inside and set it on top of the Jaguar.

Kelly suddenly "freaked out" and "jumped out of her skin," Megan recalled.

They all then returned to the house and made small talk. They discussed going upstairs to watch a movie in the couple's media room.

By now, Megan was scared: the weird phone conversations, the weird story whispered by Kelly, the reaction in the garage—something was definitely wrong here.

According to Megan, Kelly brought Megan back into the garage, just the two of them. By now it was about 1 a.m. Wednesday. While in the garage, Kelly wondered aloud why the posing lights were still on. Kelly said she normally turned them off after posing in front of them. She acted strangely dumb. She said she wished she could reach them to turn them off, but Craig's truck was parked too close. Only the truck wasn't, and the switch was within reach.

Megan didn't know what to think.

After the second trip to the garage, the two couples gathered upstairs. Rather than watch a movie, Craig had a show of his own.

He asked if anybody knew how you could strangle somebody. Not knowing what to say, Megan answered no.

So Craig demonstrated on her. He put his powerful bodybuilder arm around her with a giant bicep pressed up against her neck from behind. She instantly stopped breathing. Terror gripped her.

According to Megan, that's when Craig said that this was how he'd killed Melissa.

Craig said that it had started out as a joke, that he was fooling around with her, but then he'd strangled her.

Megan didn't know whether Craig was serious because he laughed as he said this.

"We're really going to miss her," Craig said. "I wish that it didn't have to go down like this."

But because it did, Craig added, he had to do something about it. He told Megan and Jeremy that Melissa's body was in the trunk of the Jaguar in the garage and that within hours he planned to drive the Jaguar out to Red Rock, scatter Melissa's clothes and torch the car, to make it look like she was a rape victim.

Then he said that something else—he wouldn't say what—would happen at 5 a.m., then again at 11 p.m., then again at 4 a.m.

Finally, after all this crazy talk, Megan and Jeremy got ready to leave. It was by now 2 or 2:30 a.m. on Wednesday, December 14. Megan and Jeremy had just endured three of the most bizarre hours of their lives.

As they walked toward the front door and said their goodbyes, Craig stopped them.

"Hey, wait, you forgot this," Craig said, pointing to a Nike gym bag sitting next to Megan's purse.

"What is it?" asked Megan.

"Oh, don't worry about it. I talked to Jeremy about it," Craig said. "He said it was OK to have it at your house for a couple of weeks."

Craig said the police would be coming to the house the next day and he didn't want them finding whatever was in the bag. The couple took the bag, but didn't look inside. They drove home.

Despite all they'd heard, and all the fear they felt, they didn't call police that morning. Megan claims she was deathly afraid of what Craig might do if she called them. They needed time to think.

THE NEXT DAY, THURSDAY, DECEMBER 15, CRAIG left messages on Megan's cell phone, saying that the couple were headed out of town, leaving for Greece or Mexico, Megan told the detective. Each time Megan called them back at home, the phone appeared to have been turned off.

The phone calls from Craig continued into Friday. When they finally spoke, Craig acted casual at first, as if the bizarre events of two nights earlier had never happened. He told Megan he was just calling to say hello and see what was going on.

Then he said he didn't want to speak further on the phone. He asked if he and Kelly could meet Megan in person. He suggested a Coco's restaurant on Tropicana near the 215 freeway, according to Megan.

Megan agreed, but Jeremy told her he didn't want her to go. He thought it was too dangerous. She called it off.

Later that Friday evening, Megan got another phone call, this time from Kelly, asking again if they could meet. Now Kelly suggested the home of the couple's friends and business partners in the clothing store, Greg and Diana Ruiz.

Feeling this would be safer, Megan and Jeremy went. Megan told herself the only reason she was going was to say goodbye to Kelly.

The house was buzzing with activity. Among those there were the Ruizes and Craig and Kelly. Later, Anthony Gross showed up with friend Jeff Schwimmer.

This would be another strange and scary evening.

Kelly was upstairs, "just playing dumb," Megan recalled. Kelly was saying that even though police thought the couple had killed Melissa, they would get on with their life in Greece. Kelly said she could even compete there.

Craig joined in the conversation at some point, telling Megan that he planned to sell his two houses, the one where the couple lived and the property being rented to Mandy Polk and her boyfriend, Ryan.

Craig asked Megan, a mortgage broker, if she could get quick appraisals that weekend, an almost impossible task in the red-hot Las Vegas real estate market. Megan said she would try, but made no promises.

Then Craig said something that left Megan reeling.

He said that he and Kelly needed two witnesses to say that Melissa had overdosed in the front seat of the car and the couple would get off, according to Megan.

"Absolutely not!" Jeremy said, shaking his head.

"No, no, no, we don't mean for you guys to do it," Kelly said.

But Megan didn't believe her. Upset, she went downstairs, calling random people on her cell phone just to have something to do and to get away from the madness upstairs.

Kelly came down and sat next to Megan at the dining room table.

Kelly was crying.

"Would you please stay with me a little bit longer?" she pleaded.

Megan agreed, but just for a few more minutes.

This had all gone on too long.

Finally, Megan and Jeremy left, never to see Craig and Kelly again.

AS MEGAN FINISHED THE INTERVIEW, DETECTIVE Dean O'Kelley and his team combined what she had just told him with what police already knew. If she was telling the truth—and the autopsy supported her—Megan's statement could be used to prove that Craig Titus had killed Melissa James by strangling her after Kelly had Tasered Melissa and injected her with morphine. Her account was corroborated by the forensic evidence, which had not yet been made public, showing a possible ligature around Melissa's neck and high levels of morphine in her body.

Megan was the first to relate that Kelly had said anything about using the weapon on Melissa. There was no forensic evidence to back this up: the fire had so ravaged the body that no Taser marks—tiny identification tags that are expelled along with the wires—would be visible.

The corroboration would be found in the Nike bag. Megan had turned it over to Detective O'Kelley during the interview at her lawyer's office. O'Kelley brought it back to the homicide office and, wearing latex gloves, he opened it.

Inside were two large elastic exercise bands with handles, an eight-inch-long leather blunt-force instrument—popularly known as a sap, and very illegal in Nevada—and a black molded plastic case containing an M18 Taser with two extra cartridges sealed in shrink-wrap.

CHAPTER TWENTY-TWO

ANDREW HINZ, THE LAW ENFORCEMENT TECHNICAL coordinator for Taser International, is in charge of analyzing any of the company's weapons involved in police investigations. He knows everything there is to know about a Taser, including how it feels to be zapped by one. He has been Tasered four times.

Arriving at his office via overnight mail from the Las Vegas Metropolitan Police Department in early January 2006 was a package sealed with evidence tape containing the M18 Taser, the consumer version of the M26 used by cops. It had been mailed to him by Sergeant Rocky Alby of the Las Vegas Metro Police.

Though not as powerful as the law enforcement model, the M18 is still a nasty piece of work. When the trigger is pulled, compressed nitrogen blasts out two fifteen-foot strands of wire with a pair of Number 2 fish hooks that grab on to whatever they hit, usually somebody's clothes. Eight AA batteries generate an awesome 50,000-volt shock to the victim for five seemingly forever seconds, causing what is called the "NMI Effect," for neuromuscular interference.

The victim is essentially paralyzed at the target area for a few moments. The shock disrupts the brain's electrical signals to the muscles, freezing that muscular group during those five seconds, before the body goes back to normal. The shooter can fire the device six times in a row.

Examining the model from the Las Vegas police, Hinz test-fired it on January 4, 2006—it worked fine—and noted the serial number, C1-001492, which he checked against the company's records. Although the M18 is legal, the purchaser must register the weapon by submitting a driver's license, address and telephone number. According to the files, this unit was delivered from the manufacturer to Fox's Spy Outlet, a California-based chain that has a store in Las Vegas.

The registration for this unit was mailed from the Vegas store in October 2005. It was registered to a Ryan Chastain, who police knew as the boyfriend of Mandy Polk.

Police would question Ryan, who said that the day he arrived in Las Vegas to move into Craig and Kelly's rental house, he'd spoken to Craig on his cell phone. Ryan had just pulled into the city and was lost. He got directions from Craig to the house.

That's when Craig asked him for a favor.

"He asked if I would stop by and pick something up for him," Ryan said.

Craig asked Ryan to go into Fox's store, which happened to be right around the corner from where Ryan was on East Tropicana, and buy a Taser, which he did, on his his Bank of America credit card, along with two extra cartridges. Although Ryan explained to the clerk that the gun was for somebody else, he was instructed, as the one paying for the gun, to fill out registration forms. He put down his Louisiana driver's license number and cell phone number.

Ryan then met Craig at a Chevron around the corner from Craig's house, and followed him home. Ryan said Craig had opened the Taser package, inspected the weapon and "was thoroughly excited about it and happy that he had what he wanted."

Ryan told police that he was uncomfortable with having the weapon registered in his name. "I didn't want any ownership of it. I wanted him to take care of that paperwork," said Chastain, and he asked Craig to do it. But it never happened.

Three months later, the Taser was linked to a murder case. (Police believed the story, and no charges were filed against Ryan Chastain.)

AFTER LOOKING UP THE REGISTRATION HISTORY, Andrew Hinz then downloaded the data from the internal calendar/clock in the M18. Little-known to the public, a Taser maintains an accurate electronic history of every time it is fired to help law enforcement in investigations just like this one.

According to Hinz, the records revealed that the weapon that Ryan Chastain says he bought for Craig Titus had been fired six times in quick succession on December 13, 2005, between 2:10 p.m. and just before 2:12 p.m.

This was the day before the time police say Kelly

bought lighter fluid and before her Jaguar was found in flames with Melissa James in the trunk. It was also the same date that Kelly Ryan had said that she had Tasered Melissa James, further corroboration for Megan Pierson's statement to police.

When Hinz finished inspecting the Taser, he sealed it and shipped it back to Las Vegas, where police were busy pursuing their end of the Taser aspect of the investigation.

Another little-known feature of the Taser is that it shoots more than electricity. It also blasts out tiny "AFID tags," for anti-felon identification—thirty to forty dots in yellow, pink and clear with the serial number from the cartridge written on them.

When the Taser is fired, the tags shoot out like invisible confetti, leaving a trail of evidence. The number varies from weapon to weapon so that somebody won't know how many to pick up after shooting, even if they know to look and can find them. The clear ones can only be detected by black light.

At 1 p.m. on Thursday, January 5, a team of detectives and crime-scene analysts arrived at Craig and Kelly's house with a search warrant. The couple weren't there, of course; they were locked up in a Massachusetts jail awaiting extradition to Las Vegas to face murder charges. The warrant authorized a search for blood, shoes, clothing and Taser dots.

A locksmith opened the front door. The house appeared the same as it had three weeks earlier, when the detectives had interviewed the couple. Scouring the two-story house, police came up empty on two items on the warrant—blood and shoes of any value.

But in the downstairs living room, senior crime-scene analyst David LeMaster found four Taser tags. Searching further, he found more in the messy downstairs bedroom—Melissa's room—amid the clothing and other items strewn about, more tags in the laundry room in a canister of debris from the dryer, a single tag at the top of the stairs in the entry to the office and a final tag in the upstairs master bedroom.

In all, police found twenty-six Taser dots in yellow and pink, with two different serial numbers, F03-212678 and F03-212668. Those numbers matched the serial numbers on two of the cartridges examined by Hinz. One clear dot was found, but it didn't have a serial number on it.

Police also found a size small women's red sweatsuit with red jacket in Melissa's bedroom, with the label Hot Skins. This appeared to be the same sweatsuit that Kelly was seen wearing on the security videotape during the early morning Wal-Mart run.

Police were now ready to present the case against Craig Titus and Kelly Ryan to the district attorney.

CHAPTER TWENTY-THREE

CRAIG AND KELLY NEVER WENT TO A COUNTRY WITH a non-extradition policy. Because they went to Massachusetts instead, it was only a matter of time before they would be shipped back to Las Vegas. Extradition fights within US jurisdictions almost always end in high legal bills and courtroom defeat.

And so by early January 2006, after making their initial appearance in court, Craig and Kelly waived their right to be heard on extradition and boarded buses operated by a private prison transport company for the cross-country journey back to Las Vegas.

Kelly arrived first, on January 26. She was booked into the Clark County Detention Center's women's area. Craig arrived two days later, and was booked into the jail.

While they were en route, police had received the Taser report from the manufacturer in Arizona showing that the weapon had been fired six times on Wednesday, December 14. Prosecutors amended the murder–kidnapping complaint against the couple to include the possibility of "applying an 'Air Taser' gun to the body of Melissa James."

The wording made it only a possibility because prosecutors still couldn't say for certain how Melissa had been hurt and killed. Along with the Tasering, Craig and Kelly were accused of possibly "asphyxiating Melissa James and/or suffocating Melissa James and/or administering morphine and/or a related drug to Melissa James and/or manner and means unknown, with a deadly weapon, to-wit: an 'Air Taser' gun and/or fabric ligature and/or wire ligature and/or other unknown object."

The vagueness of the complaint offered Craig and Kelly's defense attorneys a dose of confidence leading up to the couple's first court date.

"On behalf of our client," Craig's attorney, Steven Boozang, told the AP, "he is one hundred percent not guilty."

ON WEDNESDAY, FEBRUARY 1, CRAIG AND KELLY stepped into a Las Vegas courtroom for the first time. Although reporters made note of how Craig's muscles stretched his blue jail uniform, those in the bodybuilding community found him positively puny compared with the behemoth who had competed on the elite level.

Still, Craig was strong in spirit. The judge was Justice of the Peace Joseph Bonaventure Jr., whose father was the illustrious judge who'd presided over such high-profile cases as the Binion murder and the Ron Rudin killing. The younger Bonaventure read the charges against Craig, then asked if he understood them.

"Absolutely," Craig said in a firm voice.

If Craig seemed small in comparison to his competing days, Kelly looked terrible. Without her usual
makeup, hair styling, deep tan and flashy, body-hugging
clothes, she seemed run down, wan.

When Bonaventure asked her whether she understood the charges, she said in a softer, weaker voice
than her husband's, "Yes, sir."

After the hearing, the couple were taken back to
their respective cells, and their lawyers went to work.

The first order of business was to try to spring the
couple from jail until trial, with Craig's lawyers filing a
motion February 7 seeking a "reasonable bail setting"
of $250,000 instead of the no-bail hold currently in
place. Kelly's lawyer, Tom Pitaro, had told reporters
that he thought Kelly should get something closer to
the $13,000 granted to their co-defendant, Anthony
Gross, who was in home confinement.

The bail motion, filed by attorneys Richard A. Schon-
feld and Steven C. Boozang, focused in on the many
"and/ors" in the criminal complaint and declared, "In
essence, the state found Melissa James deceased and
does not have a theory as to what transpired leading up to
her death."

"Titus and Ryan went on vacation to the East Coast,"
the defense motion said.

Proving that they weren't fugitives from justice, the
defense claimed, was the fact that Kelly had left her
passport at home and that Craig didn't even have one
(although police told the media they did find one). And
although the arrest warrants were issued on December
20, Craig never knew about them until December 23,
"just hours before he was arrested." He found out by

happenstance, when talking to a prospective lawyer, Daniel Albregts, of Las Vegas, after sending the attorney a check for $5,000.

"Clearly, somebody that was planning on fleeing would not send a $5,000 retainer to counsel in Las Vegas," said the papers.

Even the couple's actions in Massachusetts suggested they had no notion they were being pursued. The bail motion attached a statement from the manager of the Jiffy Lube in Canton, Massachusetts, talking about how the couple had gotten their truck's oil change in the same bay as a trooper, and how Craig was so honest, he'd returned to pay for a lint roller he had inadvertently taken.

"The manager thanked Craig for his honesty and was extremely surprised," said the papers.

Addressing the key legal point—whether Craig was a threat to flee or to hurt anybody if let loose on bail— the papers said that prosecutors had not alleged, much less proven, that Craig was a danger to the community. It noted that he had ties to the city and Los Angeles— three years in Vegas, seven in LA—and that he owned his home and rental properties in Vegas. What's more, the papers said, Craig would have a hard time slipping away.

"Mr. Titus," the papers say, "has been featured on 97 magazine covers."

In their response, prosecutors argued that the two should continue to be held without bail, contending the evidence is strong that they'd committed first-degree murder. The couple's own statements—and lies—to police were proof of that, the prosecution said, bolstered by the surveillance video showing the lighter fluid purchase and the evidence that a Taser had been fired the day the body was found.

The prosecutors also said the couple were a flight risk, based on their statements to friends that they would be going to a country with a non-extradition policy.

"Defendant Craig Titus' motion for a reasonable bail setting is disingenuous and belied by their actions and statements," the motion said noting their efforts to sell their homes, spending the night with friends and in a Holiday Inn and driving across country with $8,300 hidden in the truck. "Obviously, these actions belie the notion that defendants simply 'went on vacation to the East Coast' as defense counsel suggests. There is, therefore, no amount of bail this court can set to ensure their future appearances."

EMOTIONS RAN HIGH WHEN CRAIG AND KELLY appeared for their bail hearing on Friday, February 10, before Justice of the Peace Bonaventure.

When he saw his wife walk in shackled, Craig broke out in tears, though his sadness seemed to turn to frustration and anger as prosecutor Robert Daskas previewed what he called the "overwhelming evidence" that they'd drugged, Tasered and then torched Melissa James because she had been stealing from them.

As if killing her weren't enough, the prosecutor said, Craig had then had the audacity to tell Melissa's mother that her daughter had faked her death, giving Maura James a "glimmer of hope" that her daughter had survived.

"What does that say about Craig Titus' character?"

asked Daskas, who continued to argue that the couple should be held without bail.

Craig's and Kelly's attorneys previewed their defense theories, including the contention that the prosecution still couldn't prove that a murder had even been committed. What's more, they said, what little evidence the prosecution had against the couple rested on witnesses with shaky credibility, including one who was a "chronic marijuana smoker" and another who was glad Craig was in jail so he could take over his business. The attorneys didn't name the witnesses.

After hearing the arguments, the judge postponed making a decision on bail. He wanted to wait until the preliminary hearing, set for March, when the prosecution would present a portion of its case to determine whether there was sufficient evidence for a trial.

But there would be no preliminary hearing. Rather than play their hand so soon in the case, and perhaps to protect vulnerable witnesses from early exposure (and cross-examination), the prosecution opted against a preliminary hearing and took its case before a grand jury.

CHAPTER TWENTY-FOUR

THE WITNESS SPOKE SOFTLY.

"Pull the mike right up close to you, if you would, please," the foreman asked.

The witness complied, and Deputy District Attorney Robert Daskas brought the painful memories flooding back.

"Did you have a daughter in December of 2005 who lived here in Las Vegas?"

"Yes," Maura James answered.

"What's her name?"

"Melissa James."

In a dress rehearsal for the trial, the Clark County prosecutor called as his first grand jury witness the mother of the victim. Maura James' testimony on Thursday, March 2, 2006, did little to implicate Craig Titus and Kelly Ryan in Melissa's death—she mainly provided time-line material—but her appearance before jurors provided an early emotional punch, putting a human face on the toll of what prosecutors were calling a murder.

In going to a grand jury, prosecutors followed a practice common in high-profile cases. The grand jury route meant that the case would be presented behind closed doors—and with no defense attorneys present—to a panel that would ask token questions and be virtually guaranteed to issue an indictment on murder charges.

As the first witness, Maura James established what prosecutors would claim was the last time anybody but Craig and Kelly had spoken to Melissa before her death. Maura recounted her cell phone call the morning of Wednesday, December 14, 2005, when Melissa phoned from the Kentucky Fried Chicken to talk about her travel plans.

"How would you describe your daughter's tone or demeanor during that telephone call?" asked Daskas.

"Her usually upbeat self," Maura said.

She spoke of going to the airport and not finding Melissa, of her phone calls to Craig that went unreturned for days. Eventually, he called back on December 17.

"He first told me that he didn't return my calls because he was out of town and didn't have that particular phone with him," Maura said. "And then he said that the police had spoken to him and that he didn't have anything to do with it. And he also said that he didn't believe it was her in the trunk of the car and that he felt like she staged the whole thing to get herself a new identity."

She could not hide her disgust at Craig, telling jurors that he'd even had a message for Melissa when she finally emerged: "He wasn't mad at her for burning the car—that he could get the money back through the insurance company," Maura said.

"As of December 17, 2005, had you been informed

with any certainty that it was your daughter Melissa James who was found in the trunk of the car?"

"No," said Maura, "there was no immediate identification."

"I have no additional questions," the prosecutor said.

HAVING BOTH HUMANIZED THE VICTIM AND SULLIED Craig's character, prosecutors offered a gruesome picture of what had become of Maura's daughter, calling volunteer fireman Dick Draper to describe putting out the car fire on the cold, dark December morning and discovering the body.

"Basically [I saw] the head and one hand and it looked like a shirt," said Draper. "I assumed it was a male. I didn't go any further than just looking."

Senior crime-scene analyst Jessie Sams gave a more detailed description of the corpse, narrating for the grand jury a series of grisly photographs that one day might be shown to Craig and Kelly's jury in open court.

"Body was folded up," Sams said. "The head was to the right side of the vehicle—or the passenger side—and knees were bent, folded up, and the feet were to the left side of the vehicle—or the driver's side—and the chest was sort of turned facing up a little bit with the left arm sort of bent under the body and the head was covered so you couldn't see the face."

Showing photos that gave an even closer look, Sams described the fleece fabrics around the head in purple, blue and black, and another in the tiger print, and how the flames had decimated the body, with only the victim's left arm and left pelvic area preserved.

When Deputy District Attorney Becky Goettsch

asked if Sams had found anything else unusual on the body, the analyst said, "It looked like there was a wire that was like in the neck area."

Turning to the police investigation, Goettsch called Detective Robert Wilson to recount his interview with Kelly Ryan later that morning, and how Kelly had immediately assumed that the victim was their live-in employee Melissa James.

Kelly, he told the grand jury, described Melissa as anything but "her usually upbeat self" in the hours before the fire, claiming that she'd had drug and theft problems that caused so much tension in the house that Kelly didn't mind dropping off Melissa at the mini-mart instead of the airport.

"I think that their relationship had been strained to the point where I don't think she [Kelly] cared where she was taking her," said Wilson. "She just didn't want her around her anymore, and neither wanted to be around each other."

The grand jury proceedings adjourned for a week, resuming on Thursday, March 9, 2006, with the testimony of another police detective, Cliff Mogg, who described his interview with Craig Titus, who'd also accused Melissa of drug use and theft, but said that Melissa and Kelly had settled their differences after Melissa spent the night in the motel.

Although it had been widely reported, prosecutors didn't ask Mogg about Craig's admission of having an affair with Melissa.

Grand jurors next saw the Wal-Mart security video pictures of the woman looking very much like Kelly Ryan purchasing lighter fluid, then getting into a

Jaguar-like vehicle in the parking lot with a man looking very much like Craig Titus. The store's asset protection employee Robin Peterson said the images were captured at 3:31 a.m.—about a half-hour before the time Dick Draper had gotten the fire call.

After a second round of forensic testimony— another crime scene-analyst, Marnie Carter, gave an even more detailed description of the body with the apparent ligature around the neck—prosecutors called one of the most important witnesses in the case, Kelly's close friend Megan Pierson.

Just 25 years old, Megan found herself testifying in a case that could send Kelly to prison for life. After describing her history with Kelly, from when Kelly had helped her recover from a broken back, through their training sessions together at Kelly's house, Megan made clear how close the two had become.

"Best friend. She was supposed to be my maid of honor," Megan, who had married in February, when Kelly was in jail, said under questioning from prosecutor Goettsch.

"In light of that," Goettsch said, "how do you feel about being here today?"

"Very upsetting," she said, grasping for words. "It's very depressing. Just not— I didn't think— I thought I knew her better than this."

In fact, she acknowledged, she didn't tell police everything she knew in her first interview.

"At first I was protecting Kelly," she said.

"Why was that?"

"Um, I believed that the things that I was told about Melissa were true, and . . . I found that they're not, so I was just being naïve, and tried to protect her in a way that I didn't think that what I was holding back really mattered."

Eventually, she did tell everything, which she repeated for the grand jury: the account of spending the evening with her then-fiancé at Craig and Kelly's house the night before the car fire, when the couple accused Melissa of drug abuse and theft, before Kelly admitted in a hushed voice that she had Tasered Melissa.

"She turned on the Taser to use it and that it, I guess, stunned her in the back of her neck, but she didn't have it up high enough, so it kind of just got her attention."

"Her, meaning Melissa?" asked Goettsch.

"Meaning Melissa's attention," said Megan. "And Kelly tried to do it again and she— I guess she didn't have the voltage up high enough, so she yelled for Craig, and Craig came upstairs, picked Melissa up, brought her downstairs into the living room and supposedly body-slammed her and started beating her up."

Shockingly, Melissa survived this and had taken a Xanax, before the couple injected "a whole needle of morphine into her leg," Megan told the grand jury. "[Kelly] said she was very resilient because it didn't do anything to her."

Later, when they all went into the garage, and Kelly had seemed jumpy when Megan's fiancé touched the Jaguar, all Megan wanted to do was get out, she said.

"I was very freaked out," she said. "I was very scared. You could just tell by the energy that something was not right, that something had gone on in there."

The evening got worse, she said, when Craig demonstrated his strangulation technique on Megan.

"He said that he was joking around, but that is how he had killed Melissa," said Megan, "by strangling her."

"Did you take him seriously at that time?"

"No."

"Why is that?"

"His demeanor," said Megan. "At times, he's very, very hard to read, you never know if he's serious or joking, and I mean, he was laughing, so I really did not believe he was serious."

The night had ended with Craig giving her fiancé the Nike gym bag that held the Taser. She said she'd given that bag to police.

Describing her next encounter with Craig and Kelly, Megan recounted the evening at the Ruizes' house that following Friday, when the couple had said they were headed for a country without an extradition policy.

The questioning ended with the prosecutor trying to establish that, as bizarre as the night before the fire was, Megan had been thinking clearly.

"Did you do any drugs or alcohol at their house either on the thirteenth or fourteenth?"

"No," she said.

"Thank you."

The next witness, lead investigator Detective Dean O'Kelley, confirmed that the gym bag had in fact contained a Taser, among other things—including a sap, an exercise rope and Taser cartridges—and that the weapon had been sent to the manufacturer for analysis.

That analysis, said another witness, Andrew Hinz of Taser International, showed that the M18 Taser had been fired six times on December 13, 2005, at 2:10 a.m., around the same time that Kelly claimed Melissa was at their house packing haphazardly for a trip Kelly desperately wanted her to take—and about fourteen hours before Melissa's body was found in the burning Jaguar. Hinz also noted that the Taser fired more than just electricity—it also sent out little multicolored tags imprinted with a traceable serial number.

Under questioning from a grand jury, Hinz could not address a critical issue in the case: whether the Taser blasts could have been lethal.

"I couldn't answer that question with any accuracy," he said. "I just interpret the data downloads and how the unit is functioning. As to the medical aspects, I'm not the person to ask or to comment on that."

Lethal or not, that Taser, according to the next witness, crime-scene analyst David LeMaster, was fired in Craig and Kelly's house. A search on January 5 turned up twenty-six Taser dots in yellow, pink and clear with serial numbers matching the model in the gym bag.

After another week-long break, jurors returned on Thursday, March 16, 2006, to hear David Levinson of Integrity Chrysler Jeep Dodge describe how a "fatigued," "skittish" and "a little jittery" Craig asked to trade in his hot rod–style Dodge SRT10 quad cab truck on Saturday, December 17, 2005, for what Levinson said was "something that could go through some rough terrain," eventually driving off with a new 2006 Dodge Mega Cab pickup.

From there, the presentation abruptly shifted to forensic evidence—and the weakest part of the prosecution's case: the cause of death. Coroner Piotr Kubiczek brought grand jurors through the autopsy, explaining that over 70 percent of Melissa's body was charred.

While he had found the wire around her neck, duct tape across her mouth, and a potentially lethal morphine level in her body, he couldn't say for certain whether she had been killed by asphyxiation, drug overdose or fire, and he found no surviving evidence that she had even been Tasered.

"Were you able to reach a determination regarding the cause of death?" prosecutor Robert Daskas asked.

In a word the defense would later seize upon, the coroner said simply, "No."

Detective O'Kelley returned to recount his interview with Anthony Gross, who told of being called by Craig early the morning of Wednesday, December 14, meeting with Craig and Kelly at the Shell station—the security video timed it at 4:12 a.m.—then going out to the desert, where the car was torched. O'Kelley also said that police obtained video from the Green Valley Grocery where Kelly said she'd dropped off Melissa on the way to the airport, but the video showed no trace of the women, or the Jaguar, around that time.

"Did you obtain additional video evidence from Green Valley Grocery store?" asked Daskas.

"Yes we did," O'Kelley said. "That was following an interview that I conducted with Craig Titus in Boston. There was an indication—"

"Let me stop you," said Daskas. "I don't want to get into the substance of any interview other than what was already admitted."

It was the first indication that prosecutors felt they had enough evidence to indict Craig and Kelly based only on their first statements to police—and that grand jurors would know nothing about the couple's change in story to admitting that they'd burned the car with Melissa in it after finding her dead of an overdose.

Instead, the questioning shifted to the surveillance video at the Green Valley Grocery taken the morning of the car fire, when somebody who O'Kelley said looked very much like Anthony Gross was in the store just minutes after Kelly had purchased lighter fluid across the street at the Wal-Mart.

O'Kelley next brought grand jurors through the phone call records, focusing on the numerous calls between Craig and Anthony the day before and the day of the fire, including several calls in the approximately ninety minutes before the blaze.

The three consecutive Thursdays of grand jury proceedings wrapped up with testimony from friends of Craig and Kelly's, starting with Ryan Chastain, then-boyfriend of Kelly's friend Mandy, who spoke of how he'd bought—at Craig's direction—the Taser reportedly fired at Melissa.

Mandy Polk followed him to the witness stand to deal the final blow to Craig and Kelly, describing how, on the day after the car fire, Kelly had told her about finding Melissa dead and then burning the body.

"She said, 'I'm fucked,'" Mandy told the grand jury, because Kelly had purchased lighter fluid on her credit card at Wal-Mart. "She and Craig decided it was the best idea to get rid of the body because, you know, she was trying to move forward with her career. She already felt like they had taken a couple steps back, you know?"

Mandy's account conflicted with Kelly's initial statement to police, making her look like a liar. Since prosecutors didn't introduce the couple's subsequent statements from Massachusetts, the panelists didn't know that Craig and Kelly themselves had ultimately admitted to what Mandy had said.

CHAPTER TWENTY-FIVE

IT TOOK THREE MONTHS FOR THE CORONER TO RE-
lease the body of Melissa James to her family. The remains were flown from Las Vegas to Tallahassee,
Florida, then driven to a Panama City funeral home.
For Melissa's final trip home, her family got hit with
the transport bill.

The funeral was held on March 16, 2006, in the
town where she'd grown up, Lynn Haven. The service
and internment, with tears and remembrances, offered
a stark reminder that Melissa James had been so much
more than the charred remains that would be graphically described next day by the coroner in the then-
ongoing grand jury proceeding.

In Melissa's obituary in her hometown newspaper,
The News Herald, the family remembered her as "a de-
voted daughter, sister, aunt and friend," and said that
"Heaven received another angel" when Melissa was
"tragically taken from us."

The obit cited this Bible passage from the second
book of Timothy: "There is laid up for me a crown of

righteousness which the Lord the righteous Judge will award me on that day."

Across the country, justice of a more worldly sort was being dispensed. On Thursday, March 23, 2006, prosecutor Robert Daskas told grand jurors in Craig and Kelly's case that "the state has concluded its evidence in this matter," and the panelists retired for deliberations. Weighing the one-sided evidence, they had a decision that same day.

"Mr. District Attorney," the foreman announced, "by a vote of two or more grand jurors, a true bill has been returned against defendants Craig Michael Titus, Kelly Ann Ryan and Anthony Gross, charging the crimes of murder with use of a deadly weapon, kidnapping, accessory to murder and third-degree arson. We instruct you to prepare an indictment."

The foreman had misspoken. In fact, Anthony Gross was charged only with arson and accessory to murder for his admitted role in helping dispose of the body. But the foreman was correct about Craig and Kelly. The most famous couple in bodybuilding and fitness were headed to trial on murder charges.

On Tuesday, April 18, 2006, the couple appeared before a new judge, District Judge Jackie Glass. Their lawyers again asked for bail, repeating their contention that the case was so weak, the prosecutors didn't even know the "means and manner" of Melissa's death. The prosecution responded that any confusion was due to the havoc that Craig and Kelly had wreaked on Melissa's body, leaving the details of cause unclear.

In her first decision in the case, Judge Glass denied

bail. Craig responded with a burst of laughter. The judge ignored him.

After another three months in jail, Craig and Kelly returned to court for a pre-trial hearing. They walked into Judge Glass's courtroom on July 16 in their blue-gray jail uniforms, shackled but allowed to hold hands. Craig seemed to have aged, and was now sporting a goatee with gray in it. Kelly, her hair back in a careless ponytail, wore glasses—the first time anybody had seen her with them.

Craig was no longer laughing, but he still couldn't keep his emotions in check. When prosecutor Robert Daskas took aim at Kelly, saying, "It was Kelly her-self" who'd Tasered Melissa and injected morphine into her, Craig snapped, "No, she did not!"

The prosecutor stared down Craig and said, "Well, let's ask Mr. Titus who did it."

"I'm getting tired of him saying that," said Craig.

Craig's latest outburst prompted a rebuke from the judge, and Craig settled down.

IN NEW JERSEY, MAURA JAMES TRIED TO AVOID newspaper and Internet reports to spare herself just these sorts of details, though inevitably she would hear about them. She came to realize that the justice system quickly forgets the victims. It was all about Craig and Kelly now. If Melissa was mentioned at all, it was in the context of a dispute about the cause of death and how that did or didn't help Craig's and Kelly's cause. Melissa James was now relegated to the statutes of forensic evidence.

In time, Maura did come to wonder about the couple. "Why in the world would they throw their whole lives away?" she wondered. "For what? Now my daughter is gone and their lives are over. I talked to Melissa just a few hours prior to the time they think she might have been killed. What could have gone so wrong in those few hours? I just don't understand."

Few did. According to their statements to police, they'd dealt with Melissa's thievery and drug use by moving her into a motel overnight, then bringing her back to the house, then buying her a ticket to be with her family in the East, then driving her to the airport, but then dropping her off at a mini-mart only a short distance from the house hours before her flight, then finding her dead of an overdose, then panicking and disposing of her body in a sports car bonfire in the desert with the help of a friend, then lying to police, then fleeing.

And why? They'd wanted to avoid PR and save careers that, by all indications, had been all but over anyway.

Their own account had them making a series of decisions so awful, impulsive and nonsensical that they flew in the face of their carefully nurtured image of disciplined athletes and savvy entrepreneurs.

Authorities, of course, claim that the part the couple had left out was how they'd murdered Melissa, either by Tasering her or strangling her or injecting her with a drug overdose—or some horrendous combination of any or all of the above. But what could Melissa have done to provoke such murderous rage?

Prosecutors suggested that her death had had something to do with the couple's anger over her stealing from them, using drugs in the house and, perhaps, having an affair with Craig.

Yet the harsh impression that has emerged was that Melissa James had never seemed to mean that much to Craig Titus and Kelly Ryan. When she lived with them off and on in Los Angeles and Las Vegas, the couple had never felt strongly enough about her to introduce her to their famous friends, as Melissa had hoped. Not a single leading figure in bodybuilding recognized her name or her picture after her death. Nobody remembered her from the many parties that Craig had thrown. Her name or picture had never appeared in the volumes of stories written about Craig and Kelly in the bodybuilding magazines. Her name had never popped up in the endless chatter on the bodybuilding websites. Craig painted her as a pathetic figure, a friend with problems, ultimately an ungrateful beneficiary of the power couple's goodness. If sleeping with her had meant anything to him, it didn't go so far as to cause him to break up with Kelly. Many in bodybuilding wouldn't have been surprised if Kelly had also been sleeping with Melissa.

As the case slogged on toward trial, neither side clearly addressed Maura James' question of why: why the bad judgment, why the erratic behavior, why the seeming senselessness of it all?

Yet there was always one factor hovering in the background that could have come into play.

When Melissa James was autopsied, the coroner had found a near-lethal level of morphine in her system, and enough morphine in her hair to suggest that she was a longtime drug abuser. Craig's friend Matt Cline, one of the few in Craig and Kelly's circle to know Melissa, described her as a drug addict, and Craig and Kelly portrayed her in the same way to police.

But Melissa James wasn't the only one associated with drugs. Going back to his troubles in Texas and Louisiana with Ecstasy, through all the use of steroids and his reported rehab just months before Melissa's death, Craig Titus had long been shadowed by the specter of drugs. As Kelly's appearance and career declined, many in bodybuilding wondered if she was succumbing to more than just aging. That she and Craig had a long reputation for partying only added to the speculation about whether Kelly, too, had a drug problem.

By the end, many, if not most of Craig and Kelly's friends were said to somehow be involved with drugs. They lived with a woman they said was a drug addict. Their own lawyers claimed in court papers filed after their indictment that Megan Pierson and her boyfriend had done drugs at the home of another friend, Greg Ruiz. As proof, the defense pointed to a statement that the couple's friend, Jeffrey Schwimmer, made to police.

"They were all shooting their dope," Schwimmer said, according to defense papers. "Schwimmer stated that Meagan [sic], her boyfriend and Greg were utilizing cocaine, Xanax and OxyCondin [sic]."

The defense claim was intended to taint the credibility of both Pierson and Ruiz. "Those witnesses," the defense said, "need to be asked about their current drug usage and their drug usage at the time of the events that they are testifying about."

But it had the added effect of throwing Craig and Kelly into this population of alleged drug users. It raised questions of whether Craig and Kelly's friends had been the only ones using cocaine, Xanax and Oxy-Contin, whether Melissa James was the only one using heroin or morphine in their house, and whether drugs had contorted and escalated the events of December 2005.

In the end, it would be up to a jury to draw the inferences and connect the dots.

CHAPTER TWENTY-SIX

ON THE LAST WEEKEND OF SEPTEMBER 2007, THE bodybuilding and fitness industry put on its biggest show, the Olympia, at the Orleans Hotel in Las Vegas. Adela Garcia won her second Fitness Olympia for the women, but the big news was in the men's competition. After four second-place finishes, Jay Cutler finally toppled eight-time Mr. Olympia Ronnie Coleman to become the reigning blond Adonis of the industry.

"A new era has begun," proclaimed Dan Solomon on the *Pro Bodybuilding Weekly* radio show. Co-host Bob Cicherillo summed up Coleman this way: "He came in big, he came in ripped, he came in conditioned."

Not far away, Flyin' Ryan was caged. Kelly spent her days reading and answering mail from friends. Once a week, she could talk to Craig for thirty minutes by phone. In her letters, she told her friends she had had a religious awakening, and had turned to God to find strength. In an interview with her former fitness colleague Brenda Kelly, who visited Kelly in jail on assignment for Bodybuilding.com, said Kelly "was so positive and clear" and that she "read me Scriptures from Jesus that blessed me for coming to see her.

"Kelly doesn't view this time spent in the Clark County Detention Center in any other way except as a blessing from God," Brenda wrote. "She feels God needed her where she is for good reason. She has never felt so sure of this faith and trust in God and lives by it minute by minute, day by day."

Her faith would be tested. In August 2006, her mother Niki Ryan, 61, died of a heart attack. Niki had guided Kelly into athletics, coached her soccer team and encouraged her to lift weights for the first time. A cardiac technician at a wellness center, Kelly's mother had struggled to cope with her daughter's arrest. She had commuted between Los Angeles and Las Vegas trying to sell Craig and Kelly's home.

"One of my major concerns for Kelly was when her mother passed away, because I knew Niki and I knew how close Kelly and her mom were," says Keith Kephart. "I thought, Oh, my Lord, this is going to send her down the tubes. But I got a wonderful letter back from Kelly saying that she was allowed to go to a chapel service."

Jailers released Kelly long enough to attend a memorial for her mother down the street with her father and her brother. She was heavily guarded, but allowed to say her goodbyes.

In a separate cell in the men's jail, Craig Titus sat and stewed. This was the first time in years that neither he nor Kelly had taken part in the Olympia, either as competitors or party promoters. Just two years earlier, Kelly's frustrated rebuff at failing to take the title had dominated discussion. Now, it was as if they didn't exist. The stories were about the new men's champion and the rebound of the women's.

The silence grated on Craig. After his indictment, he fired his attorneys and hired new ones—Kelly did the same—replacing them with a defense team that struck a more combative pose than the old ones, with one lawyer now saying, "This is going to be a war." Driving the shakeup was Craig's frustration that he wasn't being allowed to speak out. And as soon as the new team was aboard, Craig gave an interview to the *Review-Journal*, denying that he'd committed murder, but saying, "I'm guilty of some very, very bad judgment."

(One of Craig's fired attorneys, Steven Boozang, released a statement saying, "I hope Craig made the right decision for the right reasons.")

To help pay for the new legal talent, Craig put his house and rental home on the market and sold his home gym, fetching $12,100 on eBay. He also began work on an audio book. Marketed on eBay with the headline "Craig Titus Tells-All from Behind Bars," the book was to feature Craig talking into a tape recorder from his cell, "exposing the dark side of bodybuilding."

"I just want to tell them about my case here. I want to tell them about bodybuilding and how corrupt and evil it is," he said in an excerpt posted online. "Let's face it: The whole sport is one big hypocrisy."

Though jail took its toll on Craig's physique, it did nothing to fend off the storms that always seemed to follow him. Just two months after the Olympia, authorities alleged that there was a convoluted jailhouse plot to assassinate three of the most important witnesses against him, Megan Pierson, her husband Jeremy and Anthony Gross.

A man named Nelson Ronald Brady Jr., who had been housed with Craig, was arrested in a sting after he allegedly paid $1,500 to an undercover detective to kill the witnesses. Police had been tipped by a jailhouse informant who claimed to have knowledge of Brady's plans and who worked with police on the sting. Craig had been secretly tape-recorded talking by phone with Brady about a book deal and screenplay, which police claimed were codes for the hits. But Craig wasn't charged, the evidence against him ambiguous at best.

At one time, this kind of allegation would have rocked the bodybuilding industry. Instead, it warranted some posts on the message boards and a shrug by the whole sport. Craig Titus was becoming old news.

"The initial concern [was that] this would be perceived as an indictment on the personality characteristics and profile of a bodybuilder," says Dan Solomon. "As the information has made itself more available, it's become more and more obvious that this is not a product of the fact that somebody was involved in bodybuilding. This is simply people who headed down a wrong track—who just so happened to be bodybuilders."

For the first time, Craig Titus—once controversial, even feared—encountered something new: pity.

"It is just kind of sad to see they went out like that," says Ron Harris. "Craig, for all his faults, he was a really good businessman. He was good at making money, good at promoting himself, he knew how to make a good living in the industry, he always had a few sponsors, he was always hustling, he wasn't lazy. I didn't get along with him all of the time—but I always respected the fact that he was a hard worker. It was sad to see him piss it all away—and her, too. No matter what happens, if they somehow get free, and I don't see that happening, they are never gonna do anything in this industry. No one is ever going to touch them."

Craig had never looked sadder than late in November 2006. In previous months, in addition to being mentioned in the witness-assassination plot, he was considered an escape risk. Craig had raised concerns when he asked a guard how to obtain a jailer uniform, and was kept under particularly close watch.

So when a man was spotted on the roof of the jail tampering with air ducts near the area where Craig was held, jailers immediately feared Craig was trying to bust out. It turned out he had nothing to do with it, but the guards didn't know that at the time.

In a chilling episode the jailers themselves videotaped, officers descended on Craig's broom-closet-sized cell to transport him to another cell. They opened the door, with one guard warning Craig that if he resisted it "will create pain and it will possibly create death."

A dazed, shirtless, big-gutted, prison-pallored Craig Titus, looking more like an armchair football fan after too many beers than a onetime world-class bodybuilder, got handcuffed, strapped to a wheeled cart and fitted with a pair of black goggles so he couldn't see.

"What's a matter?" mumbled Craig, with a bewildered, child-like expression on his face. "What the heck is going on?"

The jailers, in full combat gear, told him that they would explain later. The tape showed Craig getting wheeled through the modern jail, into an elevator and into a tiny new cell, where the goggles and restraints were removed—as was what was left of his clothing. Craig was seen flopped face down, legs up, for a strip search.

"Oh my God," he said.

The tape would eventually make its way onto the local paper's website and be broadcast on Las Vegas TV news. As harsh as it looked, even the ACLU agreed that the jailers followed proper procedures, little solace for a humiliated Craig Titus.

The tape ended with the former Bad Boy of Bodybuilding sitting naked on his bunk, spent and confused, staring straight into the camera.